Mometrix
TEST PREPARATION

Ability-to-Benefit
Test Secrets
Study Guide

DEAR FUTURE EXAM SUCCESS STORY

First of all, **THANK YOU** for purchasing Mometrix study materials!

Second, congratulations! You are one of the few determined test-takers who are committed to doing whatever it takes to excel on your exam. **You have come to the right place.** We developed these study materials with one goal in mind: to deliver you the information you need in a format that's concise and easy to use.

In addition to optimizing your guide for the content of the test, we've outlined our recommended steps for breaking down the preparation process into small, attainable goals so you can make sure you stay on track.

We've also analyzed the entire test-taking process, identifying the most common pitfalls and showing how you can overcome them and be ready for any curveball the test throws you.

Standardized testing is one of the biggest obstacles on your road to success, which only increases the importance of doing well in the high-pressure, high-stakes environment of test day. Your results on this test could have a significant impact on your future, and this guide provides the information and practical advice to help you achieve your full potential on test day.

Your success is our success

We would love to hear from you! If you would like to share the story of your exam success or if you have any questions or comments in regard to our products, please contact us at **800-673-8175** or **support@mometrix.com**.

Thanks again for your business and we wish you continued success!

Sincerely,
The Mometrix Test Preparation Team

> **Need more help? Check out our flashcards at:**
> **http://MometrixFlashcards.com/ATB**

TABLE OF CONTENTS

Introduction

Thank you for purchasing this resource! You have made the choice to prepare yourself for a test that could have a huge impact on your future, and this guide is designed to help you be fully ready for test day. Obviously, it's important to have a solid understanding of the test material, but you also need to be prepared for the unique environment and stressors of the test, so that you can perform to the best of your abilities.

For this purpose, the first section that appears in this guide is the **Secret Keys**. We've devoted countless hours to meticulously researching what works and what doesn't, and we've boiled down our findings to the five most impactful steps you can take to improve your performance on the test. We start at the beginning with study planning and move through the preparation process, all the way to the testing strategies that will help you get the most out of what you know when you're finally sitting in front of the test.

We recommend that you start preparing for your test as far in advance as possible. However, if you've bought this guide as a last-minute study resource and only have a few days before your test, we recommend that you skip over the first two Secret Keys since they address a long-term study plan.

If you struggle with **test anxiety**, we strongly encourage you to check out our recommendations for how you can overcome it. Test anxiety is a formidable foe, but it can be beaten, and we want to make sure you have the tools you need to defeat it.

1

Secret Key #1 – Plan Big, Study Small

There's a lot riding on your performance. If you want to ace this test, you're going to need to keep your skills sharp and the material fresh in your mind. You need a plan that lets you review everything you need to know while still fitting in your schedule. We'll break this strategy down into three categories.

Information Organization

Start with the information you already have: the official test outline. From this, you can make a complete list of all the concepts you need to cover before the test. Organize these concepts into groups that can be studied together, and create a list of any related vocabulary you need to learn so you can brush up on any difficult terms. You'll want to keep this vocabulary list handy once you actually start studying since you may need to add to it along the way.

Time Management

Once you have your set of study concepts, decide how to spread them out over the time you have left before the test. Break your study plan into small, clear goals so you have a manageable task for each day and know exactly what you're doing. Then just focus on one small step at a time. When you manage your time this way, you don't need to spend hours at a time studying. Studying a small block of content for a short period each day helps you retain information better and avoid stressing over how much you have left to do. You can relax knowing that you have a plan to cover everything in time. In order for this strategy to be effective though, you have to start studying early and stick to your schedule. Avoid the exhaustion and futility that comes from last-minute cramming!

Study Environment

The environment you study in has a big impact on your learning. Studying in a coffee shop, while probably more enjoyable, is not likely to be as fruitful as studying in a quiet room. It's important to keep distractions to a minimum. You're only planning to study for a short block of time, so make the most of it. Don't pause to check your phone or get up to find a snack. It's also important to **avoid multitasking**. Research has consistently shown that multitasking will make your studying dramatically less effective. Your study area should also be comfortable and well-lit so you don't have the distraction of straining your eyes or sitting on an uncomfortable chair.

 The time of day you study is also important. You want to be rested and alert. Don't wait until just before bedtime. Study when you'll be most likely to comprehend and remember. Even better, if you know what time of day your test will be, set that time aside for study. That way your brain will be used to working on that subject at that specific time and you'll have a better chance of recalling information.

Finally, it can be helpful to team up with others who are studying for the same test. Your actual studying should be done in as isolated an environment as possible, but the work of organizing the information and setting up the study plan can be divided up. In between study sessions, you can discuss with your teammates the concepts that you're all studying and quiz each other on the details. Just be sure that your teammates are as serious about the test as you are. If you find that your study time is being replaced with social time, you might need to find a new team.

Secret Key #2 – Make Your Studying Count

You're devoting a lot of time and effort to preparing for this test, so you want to be absolutely certain it will pay off. This means doing more than just reading the content and hoping you can remember it on test day. It's important to make every minute of study count. There are two main areas you can focus on to make your studying count.

Retention

It doesn't matter how much time you study if you can't remember the material. You need to make sure you are retaining the concepts. To check your retention of the information you're learning, try recalling it at later times with minimal prompting. Try carrying around flashcards and glance at one or two from time to time or ask a friend who's also studying for the test to quiz you.

To enhance your retention, look for ways to put the information into practice so that you can apply it rather than simply recalling it. If you're using the information in practical ways, it will be much easier to remember. Similarly, it helps to solidify a concept in your mind if you're not only reading it to yourself but also explaining it to someone else. Ask a friend to let you teach them about a concept you're a little shaky on (or speak aloud to an imaginary audience if necessary). As you try to summarize, define, give examples, and answer your friend's questions, you'll understand the concepts better and they will stay with you longer. Finally, step back for a big picture view and ask yourself how each piece of information fits with the whole subject. When you link the different concepts together and see them working together as a whole, it's easier to remember the individual components.

Finally, practice showing your work on any multi-step problems, even if you're just studying. Writing out each step you take to solve a problem will help solidify the process in your mind, and you'll be more likely to remember it during the test.

Modality

Modality simply refers to the means or method by which you study. Choosing a study modality that fits your own individual learning style is crucial. No two people learn best in exactly the same way, so it's important to know your strengths and use them to your advantage.

For example, if you learn best by visualization, focus on visualizing a concept in your mind and draw an image or a diagram. Try color-coding your notes, illustrating them, or creating symbols that will trigger your mind to recall a learned concept. If you learn best by hearing or discussing information, find a study partner who learns the same way or read aloud to yourself. Think about how to put the information in your own words. Imagine that you are giving a lecture on the topic and record yourself so you can listen to it later.

For any learning style, flashcards can be helpful. Organize the information so you can take advantage of spare moments to review. Underline key words or phrases. Use different colors for different categories. Mnemonic devices (such as creating a short list in which every item starts with the same letter) can also help with retention. Find what works best for you and use it to store the information in your mind most effectively and easily.

Secret Key #3 – Practice the Right Way

Your success on test day depends not only on how many hours you put into preparing, but also on whether you prepared the right way. It's good to check along the way to see if your studying is paying off. One of the most effective ways to do this is by taking practice tests to evaluate your progress. Practice tests are useful because they show exactly where you need to improve. Every time you take a practice test, pay special attention to these three groups of questions:

- The questions you got wrong
- The questions you had to guess on, even if you guessed right
- The questions you found difficult or slow to work through

This will show you exactly what your weak areas are, and where you need to devote more study time. Ask yourself why each of these questions gave you trouble. Was it because you didn't understand the material? Was it because you didn't remember the vocabulary? Do you need more repetitions on this type of question to build speed and confidence? Dig into those questions and figure out how you can strengthen your weak areas as you go back to review the material.

 Additionally, many practice tests have a section explaining the answer choices. It can be tempting to read the explanation and think that you now have a good understanding of the concept. However, an explanation likely only covers part of the question's broader context. Even if the explanation makes perfect sense, **go back and investigate** every concept related to the question until you're positive you have a thorough understanding.

As you go along, keep in mind that the practice test is just that: practice. Memorizing these questions and answers will not be very helpful on the actual test because it is unlikely to have any of the same exact questions. If you only know the right answers to the sample questions, you won't be prepared for the real thing. **Study the concepts** until you understand them fully, and then you'll be able to answer any question that shows up on the test.

It's important to wait on the practice tests until you're ready. If you take a test on your first day of study, you may be overwhelmed by the amount of material covered and how much you need to learn. Work up to it gradually.

On test day, you'll need to be prepared for answering questions, managing your time, and using the test-taking strategies you've learned. It's a lot to balance, like a mental marathon that will have a big impact on your future. Like training for a marathon, you'll need to start slowly and work your way up. When test day arrives, you'll be ready.

Start with the strategies you've read in the first two Secret Keys—plan your course and study in the way that works best for you. If you have time, consider using multiple study resources to get different approaches to the same concepts. It can be helpful to see difficult concepts from more than one angle. Then find a good source for practice tests. Many times, the test website will suggest potential study resources or provide sample tests.

Practice Test Strategy

If you're able to find at least three practice tests, we recommend this strategy:

UNTIMED AND OPEN-BOOK PRACTICE

Take the first test with no time constraints and with your notes and study guide handy. Take your time and focus on applying the strategies you've learned.

TIMED AND OPEN-BOOK PRACTICE

Take the second practice test open-book as well, but set a timer and practice pacing yourself to finish in time.

TIMED AND CLOSED-BOOK PRACTICE

Take any other practice tests as if it were test day. Set a timer and put away your study materials. Sit at a table or desk in a quiet room, imagine yourself at the testing center, and answer questions as quickly and accurately as possible.

Keep repeating timed and closed-book tests on a regular basis until you run out of practice tests or it's time for the actual test. Your mind will be ready for the schedule and stress of test day, and you'll be able to focus on recalling the material you've learned.

Secret Key #4 – Pace Yourself

Once you're fully prepared for the material on the test, your biggest challenge on test day will be managing your time. Just knowing that the clock is ticking can make you panic even if you have plenty of time left. Work on pacing yourself so you can build confidence against the time constraints of the exam. Pacing is a difficult skill to master, especially in a high-pressure environment, so **practice is vital**.

Set time expectations for your pace based on how much time is available. For example, if a section has 60 questions and the time limit is 30 minutes, you know you have to average 30 seconds or less per question in order to answer them all. Although 30 seconds is the hard limit, set 25 seconds per question as your goal, so you reserve extra time to spend on harder questions. When you budget extra time for the harder questions, you no longer have any reason to stress when those questions take longer to answer.

Don't let this time expectation distract you from working through the test at a calm, steady pace, but keep it in mind so you don't spend too much time on any one question. Recognize that taking extra time on one question you don't understand may keep you from answering two that you do understand later in the test. If your time limit for a question is up and you're still not sure of the answer, mark it and move on, and come back to it later if the time and the test format allow. If the testing format doesn't allow you to return to earlier questions, just make an educated guess; then put it out of your mind and move on.

On the easier questions, be careful not to rush. It may seem wise to hurry through them so you have more time for the challenging ones, but it's not worth missing one if you know the concept and just didn't take the time to read the question fully. Work efficiently but make sure you understand the question and have looked at all of the answer choices, since more than one may seem right at first.

Even if you're paying attention to the time, you may find yourself a little behind at some point. You should speed up to get back on track, but do so wisely. Don't panic; just take a few seconds less on each question until you're caught up. Don't guess without thinking, but do look through the answer choices and eliminate any you know are wrong. If you can get down to two choices, it is often worthwhile to guess from those. Once you've chosen an answer, move on and don't dwell on any that you skipped or had to hurry through. If a question was taking too long, chances are it was one of the harder ones, so you weren't as likely to get it right anyway.

On the other hand, if you find yourself getting ahead of schedule, it may be beneficial to slow down a little. The more quickly you work, the more likely you are to make a careless mistake that will affect your score. You've budgeted time for each question, so don't be afraid to spend that time. Practice an efficient but careful pace to get the most out of the time you have.

Secret Key #5 – Have a Plan for Guessing

When you're taking the test, you may find yourself stuck on a question. Some of the answer choices seem better than others, but you don't see the one answer choice that is obviously correct. What do you do?

The scenario described above is very common, yet most test takers have not effectively prepared for it. Developing and practicing a plan for guessing may be one of the single most effective uses of your time as you get ready for the exam.

In developing your plan for guessing, there are three questions to address:

- When should you start the guessing process?
- How should you narrow down the choices?
- Which answer should you choose?

When to Start the Guessing Process

Unless your plan for guessing is to select C every time (which, despite its merits, is not what we recommend), you need to leave yourself enough time to apply your answer elimination strategies. Since you have a limited amount of time for each question, that means that if you're going to give yourself the best shot at guessing correctly, you have to decide quickly whether or not you will guess.

Of course, the best-case scenario is that you don't have to guess at all, so first, see if you can answer the question based on your knowledge of the subject and basic reasoning skills. Focus on the key words in the question and try to jog your memory of related topics. Give yourself a chance to bring the knowledge to mind, but once you realize that you don't have (or you can't access) the knowledge you need to answer the question, it's time to start the guessing process.

It's almost always better to start the guessing process too early than too late. It only takes a few seconds to remember something and answer the question from knowledge. Carefully eliminating wrong answer choices takes longer. Plus, going through the process of eliminating answer choices can actually help jog your memory.

Summary: Start the guessing process as soon as you decide that you can't answer the question based on your knowledge.

7

How to Narrow Down the Choices

The next chapter in this book (**Test-Taking Strategies**) includes a wide range of strategies for how to approach questions and how to look for answer choices to eliminate. You will definitely want to read those carefully, practice them, and figure out which ones work best for you. Here though, we're going to address a mindset rather than a particular strategy.

Your odds of guessing an answer correctly depend on how many options you are choosing from.

Number of options left	5	4	3	2	1
Odds of guessing correctly	20%	25%	33%	50%	100%

You can see from this chart just how valuable it is to be able to eliminate incorrect answers and make an educated guess, but there are two things that many test takers do that cause them to miss out on the benefits of guessing:

- Accidentally eliminating the correct answer
- Selecting an answer based on an impression

We'll look at the first one here, and the second one in the next section.

To avoid accidentally eliminating the correct answer, we recommend a thought exercise called **the $5 challenge**. In this challenge, you only eliminate an answer choice from contention if you are willing to bet $5 on it being wrong. Why $5? Five dollars is a small but not insignificant amount of money. It's an amount you could afford to lose but wouldn't want to throw away. And while losing

$5 once might not hurt too much, doing it twenty times will set you back $100. In the same way, each small decision you make—eliminating a choice here, guessing on a question there—won't by itself impact your score very much, but when you put them all together, they can make a big difference. By holding each answer choice elimination decision to a higher standard, you can reduce the risk of accidentally eliminating the correct answer.

The $5 challenge can also be applied in a positive sense: If you are willing to bet $5 that an answer choice *is* correct, go ahead and mark it as correct.

Summary: Only eliminate an answer choice if you are willing to bet $5 that it is wrong.

8

Which Answer to Choose

You're taking the test. You've run into a hard question and decided you'll have to guess. You've eliminated all the answer choices you're willing to bet $5 on. Now you have to pick an answer. Why do we even need to talk about this? Why can't you just pick whichever one you feel like when the time comes?

The answer to these questions is that if you don't come into the test with a plan, you'll rely on your impression to select an answer choice, and if you do that, you risk falling into a trap. The test writers know that everyone who takes their test will be guessing on some of the questions, so they intentionally write wrong answer choices to seem plausible. You still have to pick an answer though, and if the wrong answer choices are designed to look right, how can you ever be sure that you're not falling for their trap? The best solution we've found to this dilemma is to take the decision out of your hands entirely. Here is the process we recommend:

Once you've eliminated any choices that you are confident (willing to bet $5) are wrong, select the first remaining choice as your answer.

Whether you choose to select the first remaining choice, the second, or the last, the important thing is that you use some preselected standard. Using this approach guarantees that you will not be enticed into selecting an answer choice that looks right, because you are not basing your decision on how the answer choices look.

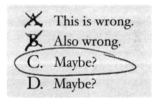

This is not meant to make you question your knowledge. Instead, it is to help you recognize the difference between your knowledge and your impressions. There's a huge difference between thinking an answer is right because of what you know, and thinking an answer is right because it looks or sounds like it should be right.

Summary: To ensure that your selection is appropriately random, make a predetermined selection from among all answer choices you have not eliminated.

Test-Taking Strategies

This section contains a list of test-taking strategies that you may find helpful as you work through the test. By taking what you know and applying logical thought, you can maximize your chances of answering any question correctly!

It is very important to realize that every question is different and every person is different: no single strategy will work on every question, and no single strategy will work for every person. That's why we've included all of them here, so you can try them out and determine which ones work best for different types of questions and which ones work best for you.

Question Strategies

⊘ READ CAREFULLY

Read the question and the answer choices carefully. Don't miss the question because you misread the terms. You have plenty of time to read each question thoroughly and make sure you understand what is being asked. Yet a happy medium must be attained, so don't waste too much time. You must read carefully and efficiently.

⊘ CONTEXTUAL CLUES

Look for contextual clues. If the question includes a word you are not familiar with, look at the immediate context for some indication of what the word might mean. Contextual clues can often give you all the information you need to decipher the meaning of an unfamiliar word. Even if you can't determine the meaning, you may be able to narrow down the possibilities enough to make a solid guess at the answer to the question.

⊘ PREFIXES

If you're having trouble with a word in the question or answer choices, try dissecting it. Take advantage of every clue that the word might include. Prefixes can be a huge help. Usually, they allow you to determine a basic meaning. *Pre-* means before, *post-* means after, *pro-* is positive, *de-* is negative. From prefixes, you can get an idea of the general meaning of the word and try to put it into context.

⊘ HEDGE WORDS

Watch out for critical hedge words, such as *likely, may, can, sometimes, often, almost, mostly, usually, generally, rarely,* and *sometimes.* Question writers insert these hedge phrases to cover every possibility. Often an answer choice will be wrong simply because it leaves no room for exception. Be on guard for answer choices that have definitive words such as *exactly* and *always.*

⊘ SWITCHBACK WORDS

Stay alert for *switchbacks.* These are the words and phrases frequently used to alert you to shifts in thought. The most common switchback words are *but, although,* and *however.* Others include *nevertheless, on the other hand, even though, while, in spite of, despite,* and *regardless of.* Switchback words are important to catch because they can change the direction of the question or an answer choice.

⊘ FACE VALUE

When in doubt, use common sense. Accept the situation in the problem at face value. Don't read too much into it. These problems will not require you to make wild assumptions. If you have to go beyond creativity and warp time or space in order to have an answer choice fit the question, then you should move on and consider the other answer choices. These are normal problems rooted in reality. The applicable relationship or explanation may not be readily apparent, but it is there for you to figure out. Use your common sense to interpret anything that isn't clear.

Answer Choice Strategies

⊘ ANSWER SELECTION

The most thorough way to pick an answer choice is to identify and eliminate wrong answers until only one is left, then confirm it is the correct answer. Sometimes an answer choice may immediately seem right, but be careful. The test writers will usually put more than one reasonable answer choice on each question, so take a second to read all of them and make sure that the other choices are not equally obvious. As long as you have time left, it is better to read every answer choice than to pick the first one that looks right without checking the others.

⊘ ANSWER CHOICE FAMILIES

An answer choice family consists of two (in rare cases, three) answer choices that are very similar in construction and cannot all be true at the same time. If you see two answer choices that are direct opposites or parallels, one of them is usually the correct answer. For instance, if one answer choice says that quantity x increases and another either says that quantity x decreases (opposite) or says that quantity y increases (parallel), then those answer choices would fall into the same family. An answer choice that doesn't match the construction of the answer choice family is more likely to be incorrect. Most questions will not have answer choice families, but when they do appear, you should be prepared to recognize them.

⊘ ELIMINATE ANSWERS

Eliminate answer choices as soon as you realize they are wrong, but make sure you consider all possibilities. If you are eliminating answer choices and realize that the last one you are left with is also wrong, don't panic. Start over and consider each choice again. There may be something you missed the first time that you will realize on the second pass.

⊘ AVOID FACT TRAPS

Don't be distracted by an answer choice that is factually true but doesn't answer the question. You are looking for the choice that answers the question. Stay focused on what the question is asking for so you don't accidentally pick an answer that is true but incorrect. Always go back to the question and make sure the answer choice you've selected actually answers the question and is not merely a true statement.

⊘ EXTREME STATEMENTS

In general, you should avoid answers that put forth extreme actions as standard practice or proclaim controversial ideas as established fact. An answer choice that states the "process should be used in certain situations, if..." is much more likely to be correct than one that states the "process should be discontinued completely." The first is a calm rational statement and doesn't even make a definitive, uncompromising stance, using a hedge word *if* to provide wiggle room, whereas the second choice is far more extreme.

11

⊘ Benchmark

As you read through the answer choices and you come across one that seems to answer the question well, mentally select that answer choice. This is not your final answer, but it's the one that will help you evaluate the other answer choices. The one that you selected is your benchmark or standard for judging each of the other answer choices. Every other answer choice must be compared to your benchmark. That choice is correct until proven otherwise by another answer choice beating it. If you find a better answer, then that one becomes your new benchmark. Once you've decided that no other choice answers the question as well as your benchmark, you have your final answer.

⊘ Predict the Answer

Before you even start looking at the answer choices, it is often best to try to predict the answer. When you come up with the answer on your own, it is easier to avoid distractions and traps because you will know exactly what to look for. The right answer choice is unlikely to be word-for-word what you came up with, but it should be a close match. Even if you are confident that you have the right answer, you should still take the time to read each option before moving on.

General Strategies

⊘ Tough Questions

If you are stumped on a problem or it appears too hard or too difficult, don't waste time. Move on! Remember though, if you can quickly check for obviously incorrect answer choices, your chances of guessing correctly are greatly improved. Before you completely give up, at least try to knock out a couple of possible answers. Eliminate what you can and then guess at the remaining answer choices before moving on.

⊘ Check Your Work

Since you will probably not know every term listed and the answer to every question, it is important that you get credit for the ones that you do know. Don't miss any questions through careless mistakes. If at all possible, try to take a second to look back over your answer selection and make sure you've selected the correct answer choice and haven't made a costly careless mistake (such as marking an answer choice that you didn't mean to mark). This quick double check should more than pay for itself in caught mistakes for the time it costs.

⊘ Pace Yourself

It's easy to be overwhelmed when you're looking at a page full of questions; your mind is confused and full of random thoughts, and the clock is ticking down faster than you would like. Calm down and maintain the pace that you have set for yourself. Especially as you get down to the last few minutes of the test, don't let the small numbers on the clock make you panic. As long as you are on track by monitoring your pace, you are guaranteed to have time for each question.

⊘ Don't Rush

It is very easy to make errors when you are in a hurry. Maintaining a fast pace in answering questions is pointless if it makes you miss questions that you would have gotten right otherwise. Test writers like to include distracting information and wrong answers that seem right. Taking a little extra time to avoid careless mistakes can make all the difference in your test score. Find a pace that allows you to be confident in the answers that you select.

⊘ Keep Moving

Panicking will not help you pass the test, so do your best to stay calm and keep moving. Taking deep breaths and going through the answer elimination steps you practiced can help to break through a stress barrier and keep your pace.

Final Notes

The combination of a solid foundation of content knowledge and the confidence that comes from practicing your plan for applying that knowledge is the key to maximizing your performance on test day. As your foundation of content knowledge is built up and strengthened, you'll find that the strategies included in this chapter become more and more effective in helping you quickly sift through the distractions and traps of the test to isolate the correct answer.

Now that you're preparing to move forward into the test content chapters of this book, be sure to keep your goal in mind. As you read, think about how you will be able to apply this information on the test. If you've already seen sample questions for the test and you have an idea of the question format and style, try to come up with questions of your own that you can answer based on what you're reading. This will give you valuable practice applying your knowledge in the same ways you can expect to on test day.

Good luck and good studying!

Sentence Skills Test

Read each sentence, inserting the answer choices in the blanks. Don't stop at the first answer choice if you think it is right, but read them all. What may seem like the best choice, at first, may not be after you have had time to read all of the choices.

ADJECTIVES GIVE IT AWAY

Words mean things and are added to sentences for a reason. Adjectives in particular may be the clue to determining which answer choice is correct.

Example:

The brilliant scientist made several _____ discoveries.

      a. dull
      b. dazzling

Look at the adjectives first to help determine what makes sense. A "brilliant" or smart scientist would make dazzling discoveries, rather than dull ones. Without that simple adjective, no answer choice is clear.

USE LOGIC

Ask yourself questions about each answer choice to see if they are logical.

Example:

The deep pounding resonance of the drums could be _____ far off in the distance.

a. seen
b. heard

Would resonating poundings be "seen"? or Would resonating pounding be "heard"?

TRANSITIONAL WORDS

Watch out for key transitional words! This can include however, but, yet, although, so, because, etc. These may change the meaning of a sentence and the context of the missing word.

Example:

He is an excellent marksman, but surprisingly, he _____ comes home empty handed from a hunting trip.

      a. often

      b. never

      c. rarely

      d. seldom

A good shot or marksman would be expected to be a successful hunter. Watch out though for the transition phrase "but surprisingly". It indicates the opposite of what you would expect, which

15

means this particular marksman must not be a successful hunter. A successful hunter would either never or rarely come home empty handed from a hunt, but an unsuccessful hunter would "often" come home empty handed, making "A" the correct answer.

TRAP OF FAMILIARITY

Don't just choose a word because you recognize it. On difficult questions, you may only recognize one or two words. Ability-to-Benefit doesn't put "make-believe words" on the test, so don't think that just because you only recognize one word means that word must be correct. If you don't recognize four words, then focus on the one that you do recognize. Is it correct? Try your best to determine if it fits the sentence. If it does, that is great, but if it doesn't, eliminate it.

ELIMINATING SIMILARITIES

Look over the answer choices and see what clues they provide. You know that three of the four will always be wrong. If there are any common relationships between the terms, then those answer choices have to be wrong.

Example:

He worked slowly, moving the leather back and forth until it was _____ .

      a. rough
      b. hard
      c. stiff
      d. pliable

In this example the first three choices are all similar. *Hard* and *stiff* are both synonyms, and *rough*, while not quite a synonym, is not the opposite of *hard* or *stiff*. Even without knowing what pliable means, it has to be correct, because you know the other three answer choices mean similar things.

FACE VALUE

When in doubt, use common sense. Always accept the situation in the problem at face value. Don't read too much into it. These problems will not require you to make huge leaps of logic. Ability-to-Benefit isn't trying to throw you off with a cheap trick. If you have to go beyond creativity and make a leap of logic in order to establish a relationship between two terms, then you should start over and find another relationship. Don't overcomplicate the problem by creating theoretical relationships that will warp time or space. These are normal problems rooted in reality. It's just that the terms that go together and the applicable relationships between the answer choices and how they fit into the sentence may not be readily apparent and you have to figure things out. Use your common sense to interpret anything that isn't clear.

READ CAREFULLY

Understand the problem. Read the terms and answer choices carefully. Don't miss the question because you misread the terms. There are only a few words in each question, so you can spend time reading them carefully. Yet a happy medium must be attained, so don't waste too much time. You must read carefully, but efficiently. Also, be sure to read all of the choices. You may find an answer choice that seems right at first, but continue reading and you may find a better choice.

Use your ear

Read each sentence carefully, inserting the answer choices in the blanks. Don't stop at the first answer choice if you think it is right, but read them all. What may seem like the best choice, at first, may not be after you have had time to read all of the choices. Allow your ear to determine what sounds right. Often one or two answer choices can be immediately ruled out because it doesn't make sound logical or make sense.

CONTEXTUAL CLUES

It bears repeating that contextual clues offer a lot of help in determining the best answer. Key words in the sentence will allow you to determine exactly which answer choice is the best replacement text.

Example:

Archeology has shown that some of the ruins of the ancient city of Babylon are approximately 500 years <u>as old as any supposed</u> Mesopotamian predecessors.

> a. as old as their supposed
> b. older than their supposed

In this example, the key word "supposed" is used. Archaeology would either confirm that the predecessors to Babylon were more ancient or disprove that supposition. Since supposed was used, it would imply that archaeology had disproved the accepted belief, making Babylon actually older, not as old as, and answer choice "B" correct.

Furthermore, because "500 years" is used, answer choice A can be ruled out. Years are used to show either absolute or relative age. If two objects are as old as each other, no years are necessary to describe that relationship, and it would be sufficient to say, "The ancient city of Babylon is approximately as old as their supposed Mesopotamian predecessors," without using the term "500 years".

SIMPLICITY IS BLISS

Simplicity cannot be overstated. You should never choose a longer, more complicated, or wordier replacement if a simple one will do. When a point can be made with fewer words, choose that answer. However, never sacrifice the flow of text for simplicity. If an answer is simple, but does not make sense, then it is not correct.

Beware of added phrases that don't add anything of meaning, such as "to be" or "as to them". Often these added phrases will occur just before a colon, which may come before a list of items. However, the colon does not need a lengthy introduction. The phrases "of which [...] are" in the below examples are wordy and unnecessary. They should be removed and the colon placed directly after the words "sport" and "following".

Example 1: There are many advantages to running as a sport, *of which the top advantages are*:

Example 2: The school supplies necessary were the following, *of which a few are*:

Arithmetic Test

A detailed knowledge of algebra and trigonometry is NOT necessary to answer to succeed on these subtests. Don't be intimidated by the questions presented. They do not require highly advanced math knowledge, but only the ability to recognize basic problems types and apply simple formulas and methods to solving them.

That is our goal, to show you the simple formulas and methods to solving these problems, so that while you will not gain a mastery of math from this guide, you will learn the methods necessary to succeed on the Ability-to-Benefit. This guide attacks problems that are simple in nature but may have been glossed over during your education.

- All numbers used are real numbers.
- Figures or drawings beside questions are provided as additional information that should be useful in solving the problem. They are drawn fairly accurately, unless the figure is noted as "not drawn to scale".
- Jagged or straight lines can both be assumed to be straight.
- Unless otherwise stated, all drawings and figures lie in a plane.

Solving for Variables

Variables are letters that represent an unknown number. You must solve for that unknown number in single variable problems. The main thing to remember is that you can do anything to one side of an equation as long as you do it to the other.

Example: Solve for x in the equation $2x + 3 = 5$.

Answer: First you want to get the "2x" isolated by itself on one side. To do that, first get rid of the 3. Subtract 3 from both sides of the equation $2x + 3 - 3 = 5 - 3$ or $2x = 2$. Now since the x is being multiplied by the 2 in "2x", you must divide by 2 to get rid of it. So, divide both sides by 2, which gives $2x / 2 = 2 / 2$ or $x = 1$.

DRAWINGS

Other problems may describe a geometric shape, such as a triangle or circle, but may not include a drawing of the shape. Ability-to-Benefit is testing whether you can read a description and make appropriate inferences by visualizing the object and related information. There is a simple way to overcome this obstacle. DRAW THE SHAPE! A good drawing (or even a bad drawing) is much easier to understand and interpret than a brief description.

Make a quick drawing or sketch of the shape described. Include any angles or lengths provided in the description. Once you can see the shape, you have already partially solved the problem and will be able to determine the right answer.

Positive/Negative Numbers

MULTIPLICATION/DIVISION

A negative multiplied or divided by a negative = a positive number.

Example: $-3 * -4 = 12$; $-6 / -3 = 2$

A negative multiplied by a positive = a negative number.

Example: -3 * 4 = -12; -6 / 3 = -2

ADDITION/SUBTRACTION

Treat a negative sign just like a subtraction sign.

Example: 3 + -2 = 3 – 2 or 1

Remember that you can reverse the numbers while adding or subtracting.

Example: -4+2 = 2 + -4 = 2 – 4 = -2

A negative number subtracted from another number is the same as adding a positive number.

Example: 2 - -1 = 2 + 1 = 3

BEWARE OF MAKING A SIMPLE MISTAKE!

Example: An outdoor thermometer drops from 42º to – 8º. By how many degrees has the outside air cooled?

Answer: A common mistake is to say 42º – 8º = 34º, but that is wrong.

It is actually 42º - - 8º or 42º + 8º = 50º

Exponents

When exponents are multiplied together, the exponents are added to get the final result.

Example: $x*x = x^2$, where x^1 is implied and 1 + 1 = 2.

When exponents in parentheses have an exponent, the exponents are multiplied to get the final result.

Example: $(x^3)^2 = x^6$, because 3*2 = 6.

Another way to think of this is that $(x^3)^2$ is the same as $(x^3)*(x^3)$. Now you can use the multiplication rule given above and add the exponents, 3 + 3 = 6, so $(x^3)^2 = x^6$

Decimal Exponents (aka Scientific Notation)

This usually involves converting back and forth between scientific notation and decimal numbers (e.g. 0.02 is the same as 2×10^{-2}). There's an old "cheat" to this problem: if the number is less than 1, the number of digits behind the decimal point is the same as the exponent that 10 is raised to in scientific notation, except that the exponent is a negative number; if the number is greater than 1, the exponent of 10 is equal to the number of digits ahead of the decimal point minus 1.

Example: Convert 3000 to decimal notation.

Answer: 3×10^3, since 4 digits are ahead of the decimal, the number is greater than 1, and (4-1) = 3.

Example: Convert 0.05 to decimal notation.

Answer: 5 x 10⁻², since the five is two places behind the decimal (remember, the exponent is negative for numbers less than 1).

Any number raised to an exponent of zero is always 1. Also, unless you know what you're doing, always convert scientific notation to "regular" decimal numbers before doing arithmetic, and convert the answer back if necessary to answer the problem.

Area, Volume, and Surface Area

You can count on questions about area, volume, and surface area to be a significant part of the Ability-to-Benefit. While commonly used formulas are provided in the actual Ability-to-Benefit test book, it is best to become familiar with the formulas beforehand. A list is provided as a special report at the end for your convenience.

Percents

A percent can be converted to a decimal simply by dividing it by 100.

Example: What is 2% of 50?

Answer: 2% = 2/100 or .02, so .02 * 50 = 1

Word Problems

PERCENTS

Example: Ticket sales for this year's annual concert at Minutemaid Park were $125,000. The promoter is predicting that next year's sales, in dollars, will be 40% greater than this year's. How many dollars in ticket sales is the promoter predicting for next year?

Answer: Next year's is 40% greater. 40% = 40/100 = .4, so .4 * $125,000 = $50,000. However, the example stated that next year's would be greater by that amount, so next year's sales would be this year's at $125,000 plus the increase at $50,000. $125,000 + $50,000 = $175,000

DISTANCES

Example: In a certain triangle, the longest side is 1 foot longer than the second-longest side, and the second-longest side is 1 foot longer than the shortest side. If the perimeter is 30 feet, how many feet long is the shortest side.

Answer:

There are three sides, let's call them A, B, and C.

- A is the longest, B the medium sized, and C the shortest.
- Because A is described in reference to B's length and B is described in reference to C's length, all calculations should be done off of C, the final reference.
- Use a variable to represent C's length, "x".
- This means that C is "x" long, B is "x + 1" because B was 1 foot longer than C, and A is "x + 1 + 1" because A was 1 foot longer than B.
- To calculate a perimeter you simply add all three sides together, so P = length A + length B + length C, or (x) + (x + 1) + (x + 1 + 1) = x + x + x + 1 + 1 + 1 = 3x + 3.
- You know that the perimeter equals 30 feet, so 3x + 3 = 30.

20

- Subtracting 3 from both sides gives 3x + 3 – 3 = 30 – 3 or 3x = 27.
- Dividing both sides by 3 to get "x" all by itself gives 3x / 3 = 27 / 3 or x = 9. So C = x = 9, and B = x + 1 = 9 + 1 = 10, and A = x + 1 + 1 = 9 + 1 + 1 = 11.
- A quick check of 9 + 10 + 11 = 30 for the perimeter distance proves that the answer of x = 9 is correct.

RATIOS

Example: An architect is drawing a scaled blueprint of an apartment building that is to be 100 feet wide and 250 feet long. On the drawing, if the building is 25 inches long, how many inches wide should it be?

Answer:

- Recognize the word "scaled" to indicate a similar drawing.
- Similar drawings or shapes can be solved using ratios.
- First, create the ratio fraction for the missing number, in this case the number of inches wide the drawing should be.
- The numerator of the first ratio fraction will be the matching known side, in this case "100 feet" wide.
- The question "100 feet wide is to how many inches wide?" gives us the first fraction of 100 / x.
- The question "250 feet long is to 25 inches long?" gives us the second fraction of 250 / 25.
- Again, note that both numerators (100 and 250) are from the same shape.
- The denominators ("x" and 25) are both from the same shape or drawing as well.
- Cross multiplication gives 100 * 25 = 250 * x or 2500 = 250x.
- Dividing both sides by 250 to get x by itself yields 2500 / 250 = 250x / 250 or 10 = x.

Simple Probability

The probability problems on the Ability-to-Benefit are fairly straightforward. The basic idea is this: the probability that something will happen is the number of possible ways that something can happen divided by the total number of possible ways for all things that can happen.

Example: I have 20 balloons, 12 are red, 8 are yellow. I give away one yellow balloon; if the next balloon is randomly picked, what is the probability that it will be yellow?

Answer: The probability is 7/19, because after giving one away, there are 7 different ways that the "something" can happen, divided by 19 remaining possibilities.

Ratios

When a question asks about two similar shapes, expect a ratio problem.

Example: The figure below shows 2 triangles, where triangle ABC ∼ A'B'C'. In these similar triangles, a = 3, b = 4, c = 5, and a' = 6. What is the value of b'?

Answer: You are given the dimensions of 1 side that is similar on both triangles (a and a'). You are looking for b' and are given the dimensions of b. Therefore you can set up a ratio of a/a' = b/b' or 3/6 = 4/b'. To solve, cross multiply the two sides, multiplying 6*4 = 3*b' or 24 = 3b'. Dividing both sides by 3 (24/3 = 3b'/3) makes 8 = b', so 8 is the answer.

Note many other problems may have opportunities to use a ratio. Look for problems where you are trying to find dimensions for a shape and you have dimensions for a similar shape. These can nearly always be solved by setting up a ratio. Just be careful and set up corresponding measurements in the ratios.

- First decide what you are being asked for on shape B, represented by a variable, such as x.
- Then ask yourself, which side on similar shape A is the same size side as x.
- That is your first ratio fraction, set up a fraction like 2/x if 2 is the similar size side on shape A.
- Then find a side on each shape that is similar.
- If 4 is the size of another side on shape A and it corresponds to a side with size 3 on shape B, then your second ratio fraction is 4/3.
- Note that 2 and 4 are the two numerators in the ratio fractions and are both from shape A.
- Also note that "x" the unknown side and 3 are both the denominators in the ratio fractions and are both from shape B.

ANGLES

If you have a two intersecting lines, remember that the sum of all of the angles can only be 360°. In fact, the two angles on either side of each line will add up to 180°. In the example below, on either side of each line, there is a 137° angle and a 43° angle (137° + 43°) = 180°. Also note that opposite angles are equal. For example, the 43° angle is matched by a similar 43° angle on the opposite side of the intersection.

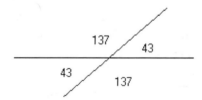

Additionally, parallel lines intersected by a third line will share angles. In the example below, note how each 128° angle is matched by a 128° angle on the opposite side. Also, all of the other angles in this example are 52° angles, because all of the angles on one side of a line have to equal 180° and since there are only two angles, if you have the degree of one, then you can find the degree of the other. In this case, the missing angle is given by 180° – 128° = 52°.

Finally, remember that all of the angles in a triangle will add up to 180°. If you are given two of the angles, then subtract them both from 180° and you will have the degree of the third missing angle.

Example: If you have a triangle with two given angles of 20° and 130°, what degree is the third angle?

Answer: All angles must add up to 180°, so 180° – 20° – 130° = 30°.

RIGHT TRIANGLES

Whenever you see the words "right triangle" or "90° angle," alarm bells should go off. These problems will almost always involve the law of right triangles, AKA The Pythagorean Theorem:

$A^2 + B^2 = C^2$

Where A = the length of one of the shorter sides

B = the length of the other shorter side

C = the length of the hypotenuse or longest side opposite the 90° angle

MAKE SURE YOU KNOW THIS FORMULA. At least 3-5 questions will reference variations on this formula by giving you two of the three variables and asking you to solve for the third.

Example: A right triangle has sides of 3 and 4; what is the length of the hypotenuse?

Answer: Solving the equation, $A^2=9$, $B^2=16$, so $C^2=25$; the square root of 25 is 5, the length of the hypotenuse C.

Example: In the rectangle below, what is the length of the diagonal line?

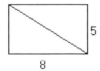

Answer: This rectangle is actually made of two right triangles. Whenever you have a right triangle, the Pythagorean Theorem can be used. Since the right side of the triangle is equal to 5, then the left side must also be equal to 5. This creates a triangle with one side equal to 5 and another side equal to 8. To use the Pythagorean Theorem, we state that $5^2 + 8^2 = C^2$ or $25 + 64 = C^2$ or $89 = C^2$ or C = Square Root of 89

CIRCLES

Many students have never seen the formula for a circle:

$(x-A)^2 + (y-B)^2 = r^2$

This looks intimidating, but it's really not:

A = the coordinate of the center on the x-axis

B = the coordinate of the center on the y-axis

r = the radius of the circle

Example: What is the radius of the circle described by: $(x+2)^2 + (x-3)^2 = 16$

Answer: Since $r^2 = 16$, r, the radius, equals 4.

Also, this circle is centered at (-2,3) since those must be the values of A and B in the generic equation to make it the same as this equation.

Final Note

As mentioned before, word problems describing shapes should always be drawn out. Remember the old adage that a picture is worth a thousand words. If geometric shapes are described (line segments, circles, squares, etc) draw them out rather than trying to visualize how they should look.

Approach problems systematically. Take time to understand what is being asked for. In many cases there is a drawing or graph that you can write on. Draw lines, jot notes, do whatever is necessary to create a visual picture and to allow you to understand what is being asked.

Even if you have always done well in math, you may not succeed on the Ability-to-Benefit. While math tests in school test specific competencies in specific subjects, the Ability-to-Benefit frequently tests your ability to apply math concepts from vastly different math subjects in one problem. However, in few cases is any of these math problems more than two "layers" deep.

What does this mean for you? You can easily learn to ace these Math sections through taking multiple practice tests. If you have some gaps in your math knowledge, we suggest you buy a more basic math textbook to help you build a foundation before applying our secrets.

Reading Comprehension

Skimming

Your first task when you begin reading is to answer the question "What is the topic of the selection?" This can best be answered by quickly skimming the passage for the general idea, stopping to read only the first sentence of each paragraph. A paragraph's first sentence is usually the main topic sentence, and it gives you a summary of the content of the paragraph.

Once you've skimmed the passage, stopping to read only the first sentences, you will have a general idea about what it is about, as well as what is the expected topic in each paragraph.

Each question will contain clues as to where to find the answer in the passage. Do not just randomly search through the passage for the correct answer to each question. Search scientifically. Find key words or ideas in the question that are going to either contain or be near the correct answer. These are typically nouns, verbs, numbers, or phrases in the question that will probably be duplicated in the passage. Once you have identified the key words or ideas, skim the passage quickly to find where the key words or ideas appear. The correct answer choice will be nearby.

Example: What caused Martin to suddenly return to Paris?

The key word is *Paris*. Skim the passage quickly to find where this word appears. The answer will be close by that word.

However, sometimes key words in the question are not repeated in the passage. In those cases, search for the general idea of the question.

Example: Which of the following was the psychological impact of the author's childhood upon the remainder of his life?

Key words are *childhood* or *psychology*. While searching for those words, be alert for other words or phrases that have similar meaning, such as *emotional effect* or *mentally* which could be used in the passage, rather than the exact word *psychology*.

Numbers or years can be particularly good key words to skim for, as they stand out from the rest of the text.

Example: Which of the following best describes the influence of Newton's work in the 20th century?

The adjective *20th* contains numbers and will easily stand out from the rest of the text. Use *20th* as the key word to skim for in the passage.

Other good key words may be in quotation marks. These identify a word or phrase that is copied directly from the passage. In those cases, the words in quotation marks are exactly duplicated in the passage.

Example: In her college years, what was meant by Margaret's "drive for excellence"?

"Drive for excellence" is a direct quote from the passage and should be easy to find.

Once you've quickly found the correct section of the passage to find the answer, focus upon the answer choices. Sometimes a choice will repeat word for word a portion of the passage near the answer. However, beware of such duplication – it may be a trap! More than likely, the correct choice will paraphrase or summarize the related portion of the passage, rather than being exactly the same wording.

For the answers that you think are correct, read them carefully and make sure that they answer the question. An answer can be factually correct, but it MUST answer the question asked. Additionally, two answers can both be seemingly correct, so be sure to read all of the answer choices, and make sure that you get the one that BEST answers the question.

Some questions will not have a key word.

Example: Which of the following would the author of this passage likely agree with?

In these cases, look for key words in the answer choices. Then, skim the passage to find where the answer choice occurs. By skimming to find where to look, you can minimize the time required.

Sometimes, it may be difficult to identify a good key word in the question to skim for in the passage. In those cases, look for a key word in one of the answer choices to skim for. Often, the answer choices can all be found in the same paragraph, which can quickly narrow your search.

Paragraph Focus

Focus upon the first sentence of each paragraph, which is the most important. The main topic of the paragraph is usually there.

Once you've read the first sentence in the paragraph, you should have a general idea about what each paragraph will be about. As you read the questions, try to determine which paragraph will have the answer. Paragraphs have a concise topic. The answer should either obviously be there or obviously not. It will save time if you can jump straight to the paragraph, so try to remember what you learned from the first sentences.

Example: The first paragraph is about radiation; the second is about cancer. If a question asks about cancer, where will the answer be? The second paragraph.

The main idea of a passage is typically spread across all or most of its paragraphs. Whereas the main idea of a paragraph may be completely different than the main idea of the very next paragraph, a main idea for a passage affects all of the paragraphs in one form or another.

Example: What is the main idea of the passage?

For each answer choice, try to see how many paragraphs are related. It can help to count how many sentences are affected by each choice, but it is best to see how many paragraphs are affected by the choice. Typically, the answer choices will include incorrect choices that are main ideas of individual paragraphs, but not the entire passage. That is why it is crucial to choose ideas that are supported by the most paragraphs possible.

Eliminate Choices

Some choices can quickly be eliminated. "Albert Einstein lived there." Is Albert Einstein even mentioned in the passage? If not, quickly eliminate it.

When trying to answer a question such as "the passage indicates all of the following EXCEPT," quickly skim the paragraph searching for references to each choice. If the reference exists, scratch it off as a choice. Similar choices may be crossed off simultaneously if they are close enough.

In choices that ask you to choose "which answer choice does NOT describe?" or "all of the following answer choices are identifiable characteristics, EXCEPT which?", look for answers that are similarly worded. Since only one answer can be correct, if there are two answers that appear to mean the same thing, they must BOTH be incorrect and can be eliminated.

> Example:
> A.) changing values and attitudes
> B.) a large population of mobile or uprooted people

These answer choices are similar; they both describe a fluid culture. Because of their similarity, they can be linked together. Since the answer can have only one choice, they can also be eliminated together.

Contextual Clues

Look for contextual clues. An answer can be right but not correct. The contextual clues will help you find the answer that is most right and is correct. Understand the context in which a phrase is stated.

When asked for the implied meaning of a statement made in the passage, immediately go find the statement and read the context it was made in. Also, look for an answer choice that has a similar phrase to the statement in question.

> Example: In the passage, what is implied by the phrase "Scientists have become more or less part of the furniture"?

Find an answer choice that is similar or describes the phrase "part of the furniture," as that is the key phrase in the question. "Part of the furniture" is a saying that means something is fixed, immovable, or set in its ways. Those are all similar ways of saying "part of the furniture." As such, the correct answer choice will probably include a similar rewording of the expression.

> Example: Why was John described as "morally desperate"?

The answer will probably have some sort of definition of morals in it. "Morals" refers to a code of right and wrong behavior, so the correct answer choice will likely have words that mean something like that.

Fact/Opinion

When asked about which statement is a fact or opinion, remember that answer choices that are facts will typically have no ambiguous words. For example, how long is a long time? What defines an ordinary person? These ambiguous words of *long* and *ordinary* should not be in a factual statement. However, if all of the choices have ambiguous words, go to the context of the passage. Often, a factual statement may be set out as a research finding.

> Example: "The scientist found that the eye reacts quickly to change in light."

Opinions may be set out in the context of words like *thought, believed, understood*, or *wished*.

> Example: "He thought the Yankees should win the World Series."

OPPOSITES

Answer choices that are direct opposites are usually correct. The paragraph will often contain established relationships (when this goes up, that goes down). The question may ask you to draw conclusions for this and will give two similar answer choices that are opposites.

> Example:
> A.) a decrease in housing starts
> B.) an increase in housing starts

MAKE PREDICTIONS

As you read and understand the passage and then the question, try to guess what the answer will be. Remember that all but one of the answer choices are wrong, and once you read them, your mind will immediately become cluttered with answer choices designed to throw you off. Your mind is typically the most focused immediately after you have read the passage and question and digested its contents. If you can, try to predict what the correct answer will be. You may be surprised at what you can predict.

Quickly scan the choices and see if your prediction is in the listed answer choices. If it is, then you can be quite confident that you have the right answer. It still won't hurt to check the other answer choices, but most of the time, you've got it!

ANSWER THE QUESTION

It may seem obvious to only pick answer choices that answer the question, but the test can create some excellent answer choices that are wrong. Don't pick an answer just because it sounds right, or you believe it to be true. It MUST answer the question. Once you've made your selection, always go back and check it against the question and make sure that you didn't misread the question, and the answer choice does answer the question posed.

BENCHMARK

After you read the first answer choice, decide if you think it sounds correct or not. If it doesn't, move on to the next answer choice. If it does, make a mental note about that choice. This doesn't mean that you've definitely selected it as your answer choice, it just means that it's the best you've seen thus far. Go ahead and read the next choice. If the next choice is worse than the one you've already selected, keep going to the next answer choice. If the next choice is better than the choice you've already selected, then make a mental note about that answer choice.

As you read through the list, you are mentally noting the choice you think is right. That is your new standard. Every other answer choice must be benchmarked against that standard. That choice is correct until proven otherwise by another answer choice beating it out. Once you've decided that no other answer choice seems as good, do one final check to ensure that it answers the question posed.

NEW INFORMATION

Correct answers will usually contain the information listed in the paragraph and question. Rarely will completely new information be inserted into a correct answer choice. Occasionally the new information may be related in a manner that the test is asking for you to interpret, but seldom.

> Example:
> The argument above is dependent upon which of the following assumptions?
> A.) Charles's Law was used

If Charles's Law is not mentioned at all in the referenced paragraph and argument, then it is unlikely that this choice is correct. All of the information needed to answer the question is provided for you, so you should not have to make guesses that are unsupported or choose answer choices that have unknown information that cannot be reasoned.

VALID INFORMATION

Don't discount any of the information provided in the passage, particularly shorter ones. Every piece of information may be necessary to determine the correct answer. None of the information in the paragraph is there to throw you off (while the answer choices will certainly have information to throw you off). If two seemingly unrelated topics are discussed, don't ignore either. You can be confident there is a relationship, or it wouldn't be included in the paragraph, and you are probably going to have to determine what is that relationship for the answer.

Time Management

In technical passages, do not get lost on the technical terms. Skip them and move on. You want a general understanding of what is going on, not a mastery of the passage.

When you encounter material in the selection that seems difficult to understand, it often may not be necessary and can be skipped. Only spend time trying to understand it if it is going to be relevant for a question. Understand difficult phrases only as a last resort.

Answer general questions before detail questions. A reader with a good understanding of the whole passage can often answer general questions without rereading a word. Get the easier questions out of the way before tackling the more time consuming ones.

Identify each question by type. Usually, the wording of a question will tell you whether you can find the answer by referring directly to the passage or by using your reasoning powers. You alone know which question types you customarily handle with ease and which give you trouble and will require more time. Save the difficult questions for last.

Final Warnings

WORD USAGE QUESTIONS

When asked how a word is used in the passage, don't use your existing knowledge of the word. The question is being asked precisely because there is some strange or unusual usage of the word in the passage. Go to the passage and use contextual clues to determine the answer. Don't simply use the popular definition you already know.

SWITCHBACK WORDS

Stay alert for "switchbacks". These are the words and phrases frequently used to alert you to shifts in thought. The most common switchback word is "but". Others include although, however, nevertheless, on the other hand, even though, while, in spite of, despite, regardless of.

AVOID "FACT TRAPS"

Once you know which paragraph the answer will be in, focus on that paragraph. However, don't get distracted by a choice that is factually true about the paragraph. Your search is for the answer that answers the question, which may be about a tiny aspect in the paragraph. Stay focused and don't fall for an answer that describes the larger picture of the paragraph. Always go back to the question and make sure you're choosing an answer that actually answers the question and is not just a true statement.

Practice Test #1

Sentence Skills

Directions for questions 1–10:

Select the best version of the underlined part of the sentence. The first choice is the same as the original sentence. If you think the original sentence is best, choose the first answer.

1. Several theories <u>about what caused dinosaurs to have extinction exist</u>, but scientists are still unable to reach a concrete conclusion.
   a. about what caused dinosaurs to have extinction exist
   b. about what caused dinosaurs to become extinct exist
   c. about the causes of the dinosaur extinction exists
   d. regarding the cause of extinction of dinosaurs exist

2. <u>Although most persons</u> prefer traditional pets like cats and dogs, others gravitate towards exotic animals like snakes and lizards.
   a. Although most persons
   b. Because most people
   c. While most people
   d. Maybe some persons

3. It is important that software companies offer tech support <u>to customers who are encountering problems</u>.
   a. to customers who are encountering problems
   b. because not all customers encounter problems
   c. with customers who encounter problems
   d. to customer who is encountering difficulties

4. The fact <u>that children eat high fat diets and watch excessive amount of television are a cause of concern</u> for many parents.
   a. that children eat high fat diets and watch excessive amount of television are a cause of concern
   b. the children eat high fat diets and watches excessive amount of television are a cause of concern
   c. is children eat high fat diets and watch excessive amount of television is a cause for concern
   d. that children eat high fat diets and watch excessive amounts of television is a cause for concern

5. <u>Contrarily to popular beliefs,</u> bats do not actually entangle themselves in the hair of humans on purpose.
   a. Contrarily to popular beliefs
   b. Contrary to popular belief
   c. Contrary to popularity belief
   d. Contrary to popular believing

31

6. Considering how long ago the Ancient Egyptians lived, it's amazing we know anything about them at all.
   a. Considering how long ago the Ancient Egyptians lived, it's amazing
   b. Consider how long the Ancient Egyptians lived, it's amazing
   c. Considering for how long the Ancient Egyptians lived, its amazing
   d. Considering, how long ago the Ancient Egyptians lived, its amazing

7. **Because technology has constantly changed**, those employed in the IT industry must learn new skills continuously.
   a. Because technology has constantly changed
   b. Because technology is constantly changing
   c. Even though technology is changing
   d. Despite the fact that technology has changed

8. **To mix, shade, and highlighting** are essential skills that every beginning artist must master.
   a. To mix, shade, and highlighting
   b. Mix, shade, and highlighting
   c. To mixing, shading, and highlighting
   d. Mixing, shading, and highlighting

9. The growing problem of resistance to antibiotics can be attributed, in part, **to the fact that they are prescribed unnecessarily**.
   a. to the fact that they are prescribed unnecessarily
   b. in the facts that they are prescribed unnecessarily
   c. to the fact that they are prescribing unnecessarily
   d. with the facts that they are being prescribed unnecessarily

10. **A key challenges facing university graduates** searching for employment is that most have limited work experience.
   a. A key challenges facing university graduates
   b. Key challenge faced by university graduates
   c. A key challenge facing university graduates
   d. Key challenges facing university's graduates

Directions for questions 11–20:

Rewrite the sentence in your head following the directions given below. Keep in mind that your new sentence should be well written and should have essentially the same meaning as the original sentence.

11. Mitosis is the process of cell division, and if there are errors during this process, it can result in serious complications.

Rewrite, beginning with:

<u>Serious complications can result</u>

The next words will be:

    a. during the process of cell division
    b. if there are errors during the process
    c. in the process of mitosis
    d. when this process leads to errors

12. It was a very tough decision, but Sharon finally decided after much consideration to study biology at Yale University.

Rewrite, beginning with:

<u>After much consideration</u>

The next words will be:

    a. Sharon finally decided to study
    b. it was a very tough decision
    c. Sharon studied biology at Yale University
    d. a very tough study was decided

13. Small business owners must compete with larger stores by providing excellent service, because department store prices are simply too low for owners of small businesses to match them.

Rewrite, beginning with:

<u>Prices in department stores are simply too low for owners of small businesses to match them,</u>

The next words will be:

    a. so small business owners must
    b. while small business owners must
    c. when small business owners must
    d. because small business owners must

14. Ants are fascinating creatures, and some of their unique characteristics are their strength, organizational skills, and construction talents.

Rewrite, beginning with:

<u>Strength, organizational skills, and construction talents</u>

The next words will be:

    a. are some of the unique characteristics
    b. are possessed by fascinating creatures
    c. of ants are fascinating characteristics
    d. are unique characteristics of their

15. Many people do not regularly wear their seatbelts, even though law enforcement professionals warn motorists about the dangers of not doing so.

Rewrite, beginning with:

Despite warnings by law enforcement professionals

The next words will be:

    a.   motorists ignore the dangers of not doing so
    b.   many people do not regularly wear their seatbelts
    c.   about the people who don't wear seatbelts
    d.   even though motorists do not wear seatbelts

16. The wolverine is an incredibly strong animal that is actually closely related to weasels, and not, as many people believe, related to wolves.

Rewrite, beginning with:

Many people believe the wolverine is

The next words will be:

    a.   closely related to weasels
    b.   an incredibly strong animal
    c.   related to wolves
    d.   a weasel, but they are actually

17. Advertising aimed at children is of greater concern than that aimed towards adults because children are more likely to internalize the messages presented in print and television ads.

Rewrite, beginning with:

Because children are more likely to internalize the messages presented in ads,

The next words will be:

    a.   advertising aimed at children
    b.   advertising aimed towards adults
    c.   is of greater concern than that
    d.   print and television advertisements

18. Increasing housing and fuel costs in the United States have caused many people to accumulate high levels of consumer and credit debt, and this is particularly true for people who have limited incomes.

Rewrite, beginning with:

Many people have accumulated high levels of debt

The next words will be:

    a.   for those who have limited income
    b.   mainly in the United States
    c.   due to increasing housing and fuel costs
    d.   for consumer and credit

19. People and companies who sell products online often charge a lot for shipping, which is why even though it is possible to find low prices online, customers may not be saving as much money as they think.

Rewrite, beginning with:

<u>Customers may not be saving as much money as they think</u>

The next words will be:

   a. which is why it is possible to charge for shipping
   b. because people and companies who sell
   c. because it is possible to find low prices
   d. when people and companies shop online

20. In the world of stock option trading, purchasing a put gives an individual the right to sell shares, so they will likely profit if the value of a company's stock decreases, but not if it increases.

Rewrite, beginning with:

<u>An individual will profit if the value of a company's stock decreases</u>

The next words will be:

   a. in the world of stock option trading
   b. giving them a right to sell shares
   c. or if it increases
   d. if he purchases a put

Reading Comprehension

Directions for questions 1–10:

Read the statement or passage and then choose the best answer to the question. Answer the question based on what is stated or implied in the statement or passage.

> During the 1970s, a new type of pet became popular in North America. Although they were actually just brine shrimp, they were marketed as "Sea Monkeys." They don't actually look like monkeys at all, but were branded as such due to their long tails. When sea monkeys first began to be sold in the United States, they were sold under the brand name "Instant Life." Later, when they became known as sea monkeys, the cartoon drawings that were featured in comic books showed creatures that resembled humans more than shrimp. The creative marketing of these creatures can only be described as genius, and at the height of their popularity in the 1970s, they could be found in as many as one in five homes.

1. Based on the information in the above passage, it can be inferred that:

   a. Sea monkeys were more popular when they were marketed as "instant life."
   b. Sea monkeys wouldn't have been as popular if they had been marketed as "brine shrimp."
   c. Most people thought they were actually purchasing monkeys that lived in the sea.
   d. There are more homes today that have sea monkeys than there were in the 1970s.

> Before the battle between CDs and MP3s, there was a rivalry during the 1960s between the four-track and the eight-track tape. Four-track tapes were invented in the early 1960s by Earl Muntz, an entrepreneur from California. Later, Bill Lear designed the eight-track tape. This latter invention was similar in size to the four-

track tape, but it could store and play twice as many songs. Lear had close ties with the motor company Ford, and he convinced them to include eight-track players in their vehicles, which definitely helped the eight-track tape to achieve a high level of popularity. Soon after, they began being used in homes, and the four-track tape all but disappeared.

2. The main difference between the four-track and eight-track tape was:
a. The four-track tape was much larger than the eight-track tape.
b. The eight-track tape cost a lot more to produce than the four-track tape.
c. The eight-track tape could hold more songs than the four-track tape.
d. The four-track tape was usually included in Ford vehicles.

It is natural for humans to have fears, but when those fears are completely irrational and begin to interfere with everyday activities they are known as phobias. Agoraphobia is a serious phobia, and it can be devastating for those who suffer from it. Contrary to popular belief, agoraphobia is not simply a fear of open spaces. Rather, the agoraphobic fears being in a place that he feels is unsafe. Depending on the severity of the problem, the agoraphobic might fear going to the mall, walking down the street, or even walking to the mailbox. Often, the agoraphobic will view his home as the safest possible place to be, and he may even be reluctant to leave his house. Treatments for this condition include medication and behavioral therapy.

3. An agoraphobic would feel safest:
a. In their yard
b. In their house
c. In a mall
d. On the sidewalk

The butterfly effect is a somewhat poorly understood mathematical concept, primarily because it is interpreted and presented incorrectly by the popular media. It refers to systems, and how initial conditions can influence the ultimate outcome of an event. The best way to understand the concept is through an example. You have two rubber balls. There are two inches between them, and you release them. Where will they end up? Well, that depends. If they're in a sloped, sealed container, they will end up two inches away from each other at the end of the slope. If it's the top of a mountain, however, they may end up miles away from each other. They could bounce off rocks; one could get stuck in a snow bank while the other continues down the slope; one could enter a river and get swept away. The fact that even a tiny initial difference can have a significant overall impact is known as the butterfly effect.

4. The purpose of the above passage is:
a. To discuss what could happen to two rubber balls released on top of a mountain.
b. To show why you can predict what will happen to two objects in a sloped, sealed container.
c. To discuss the primary reason why the butterfly effect is a poorly understood concept.
d. To give an example of how small changes at the beginning of an event can have large effects.

Wells provide water for drinking, bathing, and cleaning to many people across the world. When wells are being dug, there are several issues that must be taken into account to minimize the chance of potential problems down the road. First, it's important to be aware that groundwater levels differ, depending on the season. In general, groundwater levels will be higher during the winter. So if a well is being dug during the winter, it should be deep enough to remain functional during the summer, when water levels are lower. Well water that is used is replaced by melting snow and rain. If the well owners are using the water faster than it can be replaced, however, the water levels will be lowered. The only way to remedy this, aside from waiting for the groundwater to be replenished naturally, is to deepen the well.

5. From the above passage, it can be concluded that:

a. It is better to have a well that is too deep than one that is too shallow.
b. Most well owners will face significant water shortages every year.
c. Most people who dig wells during the winter do not make them deep enough.
d. Well water is safe to use for bathing and cleaning, but is not suitable for drinking.

Today's low-fat craze has led many people to assume that all fats are unhealthy, but this is simply not the case. Fat is an essential component of any healthy diet because it provides energy and helps the body process nutrients. While all fats should be consumed in moderation, there are good and bad fats. Good fats are what are known as unsaturated fats. They are found in olive oil, fatty fish like salmon, and nuts. Bad fats are saturated and trans fats. They are found in foods like butter, bacon, and ice cream. Consumption of foods that contain trans or saturated fats should be restricted or avoided altogether.

6. The main purpose of the above passage is to:

a. Explain why fat is important for the body
b. Discuss some of the main sources of good fats
c. Talk about the different types of fats
d. Discuss examples of foods that should be avoided

Satire is a genre that originated in the ancient world and is still popular today. Although satire is often humorous, its purposes and intentions go well beyond simply making people laugh. Satire is a way for the playwright, author, or television producer to criticize society, human nature, and individuals that he holds in contempt. Satire as we know it today developed in Ancient Greece and Rome. There were three main types. The first, Menippean satire, focused on criticizing aspects of human nature. This was done by introducing stereotypical, one-dimensional characters. Horatian satire can be viewed as gentle satire. It made fun of people and their habits, but in a way that was not offensive. Juvenalian satire was written is such a way that the audience would experience feelings of disgust and aversion when they saw the characters and their actions. Some of the most popular satires today are fake news shows, like the *Daily Show* and the *Colbert Report*, and satirical comic strips like *Doonesbury*.

7. The main purpose of the above passage is:
   a. To discuss the history of satire.
   b. To present the major types of satire.
   c. To discuss modern examples of satire.
   d. To present the purposes of satire.

Many people believe that how we express our feelings is mainly determined by our upbringing and culture. Undoubtedly, this is true in some cases. In North America, for example, it is customary to shake hands when we meet somebody to express acceptance, whereas in other countries they may simply bow slightly to indicate this. Many feelings, however, are expressed in similar ways by people all over the world. These emotions include, fear, anger, happiness, disgust, and sorrow. For example, if a person is experiencing fear, their eyes will widen and their pupils will dilate. This reaction is largely involuntary. The finding that people express many feelings in a similar manner, regardless of where they are from, indicates that facial expressions are influenced more by evolution than culture.

8. Based on the above passage, it can be concluded that:
   a. People often can't hide what they are feeling
   b. People from other parts of the world express happiness differently
   c. Fear is the only emotion that is felt by everybody in the world
   d. Acceptance is a feeling invented by man

Cities are typically warmer than the surrounding countryside, a phenomenon known as the heat island effect. There are numerous causes of this phenomenon, including emissions from cars and buildings. This creates a mini greenhouse effect. In rural areas, the standing water in marshes and ponds evaporates, which cools the air slightly. This does not occur to the same extent in the city. The tall buildings in the center of most cities block winds that would provide some relief from the excessive heat. Finally, the color and material of most roads and buildings absorbs rather than reflects heat. Although planting trees and using building materials that reflect heat may alleviate the problem somewhat, it will by no means eliminate it.

9. The main purpose of the above passage is to:
   a. Talk about how the problem of heat island can be solved
   b. Argue that cities should make an effort to plant more trees
   c. Present the major causes of the problem of heat island
   d. Contrast the city environment to that of the countryside

Marsupials resemble mammals in a number of ways. For one thing, they are warm-blooded creatures. They have hair, and the mothers feed their young by producing milk. However, one thing that separates marsupials from mammals is that their young are born when they are not yet fully-developed. Most are born after only about four or five weeks. They finish their development in the pouch of their mother. Some of the more commonly known marsupials are koalas, kangaroos, and opossums. They are a diverse group, with many members having little in common besides their reproductive traits.

10. A major difference between marsupials and mammals is:
   a. Marsupials have hair, while mammals do not.
   b. Mammals are a much more diverse group than marsupials.
   c. Marsupials are born at an earlier stage of development.
   d. Mammals feed their young by producing milk.

Directions for questions 11–20

For the questions that follow, two underlined sentences are followed by a question or statement. Read the sentences, then choose the best answer to the question or the best completion of the statement.

11. Atheists are individuals who do not believe in any type of higher power.
   <u>**Theists usually possess religious and spiritual beliefs and have faith in one or more gods.**</u>

What does the second sentence do?
   a. It states an example
   b. It makes a contrast
   c. It disputes the first sentence
   d. It offers a solution

12. Home schooling refers to the practice of educating children at home rather than sending them to school.

> **Home schooling usually involves one parent giving up their career in order to stay home.**

What does the second sentence do?

- a. It restates the information from the first.
- b. It provides an example.
- c. It states an effect.
- d. It contradicts the first.

13. Coffee is the most popular beverage in the entire world, and it is estimated that about 80% of Americans drink coffee.

> **According to a recent study, about 85% of North Americans drink soda, making it the most popular drink worldwide.**

What does the second sentence do?

- a. It makes a contrast
- b. It gives an example
- c. It supports the first
- d. It contradicts the first

14. Regeneration refers to the ability that some animals have to replace severed body parts.

> **A salamander that has had its tail chopped off can grow a new one that is practically identical to the original.**

What does the second sentence do?

- a. It restates the information from the first
- b. It provides an example
- c. It supports the first
- d. It presents a solution

15. Even though monthly rent on an apartment is usually less than a mortgage payment, most people would still rather own their own home.

> **Home ownership is a dream for most North Americans, even though monthly costs for houses are higher than those for apartments.**

What does the second sentence do?

- a. It contradicts the first
- b. It supports the first
- c. It restates the information in the first
- d. It explains the information in the first

16. Soil contamination can be caused by a wide variety of factors, including leakage from underground septic tanks.

> **Septic tanks will corrode over time, and when they leak or rupture, the contents contaminate the surrounding soil.**

What does the second sentence do?

    a. It expands on the first.
    b. It restates the information in the first.
    c. It states an effect.
    d. It proposes a solution.

17. The Richter Scale is the most commonly-used method to measure the strength of earthquakes.

> **Even though other methods are used more frequently to measure earthquakes, the Richter Scale is the most trusted.**

What does the second sentence do?

    a. It provides an example
    b. It reinforces the information in the first
    c. It contradicts the information in the first
    d. It presents a conclusion

18. Adaptation refers to the ability of an animal to change in order to be better suited for its environment and to increase its chances of survival.

> **Porcupines have sharp quills that can be used to ward off animals that might otherwise try to hunt them.**

What does the second sentence do?

    a. It expands on the information in the first
    b. It presents an example
    c. It states an effect
    d. It makes an inference

19. Congestion due to excessive traffic means that many people are forced to sit in traffic on their way to work.

> **Carpooling and public transportation can effectively reduce the number of cars on the road.**

How are the two sentences related?

    a. They explain several concepts
    b. They provide a concept and an example
    c. They support one another
    d. They state a problem and a solution

20. Men are known for being analytical when they make decisions.

> **Women often make decisions based on intuition and gut feelings.**

What does the second sentence do?

    a. It gives an example.
    b. It expands on the first.
    c. It provides a contrast.
    d. It contradicts the first.

Arithmetic Test

1. 6/12 is equivalent to which fraction?
   a. 10/24
   b. 3/4
   c. 3/6
   d. 1/6

2. 675 × 7 =
   a. 4,535
   b. 4,675
   c. 4,865
   d. 4,725

3. Which of the following is closest to 5,465 + 394?
   a. 5,000
   b. 5,500
   c. 6,000
   d. 6,500

4. 11/12 – 1/6 =
   a. 1/4
   b. 1/2
   c.   3/4
   d. 5/6

5. 743 – 87 =
   a. 626
   b. 656
   c. 674
   d. 694

6. 75 ÷ 16 =
   a. 4.69
   b. 5.23
   c. 6.05
   d. 7.39

7. 598 × 46 =
   a. 26,014
   b. 26,182
   c. 27,295
   d. 27,508

8. Which of the following is closest to 0.35?
   a. 1/4
   b. 1/3
   c. 1/2
   d. 3/5

9. 6.52 + 0.2 + 0.05 =
   a. 6.57
   b. 6.75
   c. 6.77
   d. 6.95

10. 9/5 =
    a. 0.56
    b. 0.95
    c. 1.5
    d. 1.8

11. 0.058 / 6.37 =
    a. 0.005
    b. 0.009
    c. 0.04
    d. 0.08

12. Which of the following represents the largest value?
    a. 0.0095
    b. 0.008
    c. 0.072
    d. 0.069

13. Kate got a 56 on her first math test. On her second math test, she raised her grade by 12%. What was her grade?
    a. 62.7
    b. 67.2
    c. 68.0
    d. 72.3

14. A factory can produce 12 tonnes of cereal per day. A customer has ordered 596 tonnes of cereal. How many days will it take the factory to fill the customer's order?
    a. 48
    b. 50
    c. 52
    d. 54

15. If one side of a square has a length of 56 cm, what is its perimeter?
    a. 112 cm
    b. 224 cm
    c. 448 cm
    d. 3136 cm

16. Four people decide to adopt a dog and take turns caring for it. Person A thinks he can take care of the dog 1/4 of the time; person B thinks she can handle 1/8; person C thinks he can take care of the dog 1/2 of the time. What part is left for the fourth person to cover?

    a. 1/8
    b. 1/4
    c. 1/3
    d. 1/2

17. A skyscraper is 548 meters high. The building's owners decide to increase its height by 3%. How high would the skyscraper be after the increase?

    a. 551 meters
    b. 555 meters
    c. 562 meters
    d. 564 meters

Answer Key and Explanations

Sentence Skills

1. B: The phrase *to have extinction* in choice A is grammatically incorrect. In choice C, *causes* is plural, and so the word should be *exist* rather than *exists*. D is not the best choice because it is somewhat awkward. B sounds the best and is also grammatically correct.

2. C: C is the best answer because it indicates a contrast and is grammatically correct.

3. A: A is the best answer because it denotes the party to whom companies are offering tech support and because the verb *are* agrees with the noun *customers*.

4. D: D is the best choice. The phrases *high-fat diets* and *excessive amounts of television* agree with each other because they are both plural. The word *is* refers to *the fact that*, so these also agree with each other.

5. B: This is a well-known phrase meaning *despite what most people believe*. The word *contrarily* in choice A makes it incorrect. *Popularity* in choice C is out of place, and *believing* in choice D is incorrect.

6. A: B implies the Egyptians had long life spans, which doesn't make sense in the context of the sentence. C uses *its* instead of the grammatically correct *it's*, while D has misplaced commas and also uses *its*. A indicates the Egyptians lived a long time ago, and the correct form of *it's* is used.

7. B: The sentence describes a cause/effect relationship, so *because* is the correct way to begin the sentence. Choice A implies that technology changed in the past, which does not make sense in the context of the sentence. B indicates a cause/effect relationship, and states that technology is continuously changing, which is why IT professionals must continuously learn new skills.

8. D: Choice D is correct because the three verbs are in the same form. Choices A and B use different verb forms. Choice C is grammatically incorrect because of the *to* that is used to begin the sentence.

9. A: Saying that something can be *attributed to* something else is grammatically correct, which eliminates choices B and D. C is incorrect because *they* refers to antibiotics, so the sentence is essentially stating that antibiotics are prescribing. Inanimate objects are incapable of doing this, which makes the sentence incorrect. Choice A states that antibiotics are prescribed, indicating someone else is doing the prescribing, which makes it the correct choice.

10. C: A is incorrect because *a* and *challenges* do not agree. B is incorrect because *key challenge* must be prefaced by *A* D is incorrect because of the misplaced apostrophe, and also because the sentence only identifies one challenge, meaning the plural, *key challenges*, is incorrect.

11. B: The original sentence states that serious complications can result if there are errors during the process of cell division. A and C refer to the process of cell division only, and not the errors that must be made for complications to occur. D indicates that the process leads to errors, rather than that the errors occur during the process.

12. A: The original sentence states that after much consideration a decision was made, which is why A is the best choice. The decision wasn't still difficult after much consideration, as B indicates, and

45

she didn't immediately attend university, as is indicated by C. D simply doesn't make sense in the context of the statement.

13. A: A is the best choice because it is the only one that indicates a cause/effect relationship. Small business owners must do something *because* prices in department stores are too low for small business owners to match them.

14. A: The rewritten sentence begins with examples of some of the unique characteristics of ants. B does not indicate that they are unique characteristics; C describes them as fascinating rather than unique; and D does not make sense in the context of the sentence because of the phrase *of their* that follows *are unique characteristics*.

15. B: The word *despite* indicates that something is done in spite of warnings by law enforcement professionals, which eliminates choices C and D. A does not indicate precisely what motorists are failing to do, which eliminates that choice. B is the correct answer.

16. C: The original sentence states that many people believe the wolverine is related to wolves. They are related to weasels, but this is not something many people believe, eliminating choices A and D. The original sentence describes the strength of wolverines as a fact rather than a belief, eliminating choice B.

17. A: The word *because* indicates a cause/effect relationship. Since the phrase focuses on children, choice B can be eliminated. C does not indicate what "is of greater concern," so it can be eliminated. D is basically just describing the different types of ads, essentially restating something that has already been said. Answer choice A focuses on children and identifies advertising as the focus of the sentence, making it the best choice.

18. C: C is the only choice that offers an explanation as to why people have accumulated debt. A and D cannot logically follow the introductory phrase. B was not a fact expressed in the original sentence.

19. B: A indicates shipping costs can be charged because consumers are not saving as much money as they think, which is not an idea expressed in the original sentence. C states they may not be saving as much money as they think because they can find low prices, an idea that is also not stated in the original sentence. D indicates that companies shop online, an idea not expressed in the original sentence. B indicates there is a reason why people are not saving as much as they think. It then identifies people and companies, which are also identified in the original sentence, making it the correct choice.

20. D: A is too general, indicating that an individual will always profit if a company's stock decreases. B indicates that the right to sell shares is contingent on the decrease of a company's stock, which is also not the case. C indicates the individual will profit from a decrease or an increase, but the original sentence clearly states there will be no profit if a stock increases. D tells how an individual can profit if the value of a stock decreases (by purchasing a put), making it the correct choice.

Reading Comprehension

1. B: In describing the marketing of "sea monkeys," the author describes it as creative genius, and attributes their popularity to the drawings and advertisements that appeared in comic books. It is reasonable to conclude that without the branding and (somewhat misleading) ads, they wouldn't

have been as popular. Marketing them under the less exciting brand name "brine shrimp" likely wouldn't have resulted in as many sales.

2. C: A is incorrect because the passage states they were similar in size. The cost of production is not mentioned, eliminating B as a possibility. D is incorrect because it was the eight-track tape that was included in these vehicles. C is correct because the passage states the eight-track tape could store and play twice as many songs.

3. B: The passage states that, "Often, the agoraphobic will view his home as the safest possible place to be, and he may even be reluctant to leave his house," making B the correct choice.

4. D: B and C are only briefly mentioned, allowing them to be eliminated as possibilities. Although the passage does discuss what could happen to two balls released at the top of a mountain, that is not the purpose of the passage, so A can be eliminated. The purpose is to show how small differences (in this case two inches between two rubber balls) can have large effects. This is essentially what the butterfly effect is, and the purpose of the passage is to give an example to demonstrate this principle.

5. A: The passage discusses several problems that can occur with wells. Both of the problems mentioned are associated with wells that are too shallow; no problems associated with wells that are too deep are mentioned. Therefore, it seems safe to conclude that a deeper well would be more desirable than a shallow one.

6. C: A is mentioned only briefly in the passage. B and D are mentioned, but this information does not fit into the overall purpose of the passage, which is to discuss the different types of fats, both good and bad.

7. B: C and D are mentioned only briefly. Although the history of satire is discussed, most of the passage focuses on discussing the three major forms of satire that originated in Ancient Greece and Rome, making B the best choice.

8. A: B is incorrect because the passage states that happiness is expressed similarly by people all over the world. C is incorrect because the passage states that there are many emotions felt and expressed by people all over the world. D is incorrect because, although people may express acceptance differently, that is not sufficient to conclude it is not a natural emotion. A is correct. We can conclude that people can't always hide what they are feeling because of the statement in the passage that the facial expressions associated with emotions like fear are largely involuntary.

9. C: C is the correct answer because the passage mainly focuses on discussing the causes of heat island. A, B, and D are touched upon only in passing.

10. C: A and D are incorrect because the passage states that these are characteristics that marsupials and mammals share. B can be eliminated, because it is not mentioned in the passage. C is the correct choice, as "one thing that separates marsupials from mammals is that their young are born when they are not yet fully-developed" is stated in the passage.

11. B: Theists are the opposite of atheists, so the second sentence provides a contrast to the first.

12. C: The first sentence introduces the concept of home schooling. The second sentence states that one parent usually has to give up their job for home schooling to take place, which is a direct effect of the practice of home schooling.

13. D: The first sentence states that coffee is the most popular beverage. The second sentence directly contradicts it, stating that soda is the most popular. The second sentence contradicts the first.

14. B: A salamander's ability to grow a new tail is an example of the ability to replace severed body parts, which is known as regeneration. The second sentence provides an example of the concept explained in the first.

15. C: Both sentences give the same information, and nothing new is added. The second sentence restates the information from the first.

16. A: The second sentence tells how septic tanks can contribute to the problem of soil contamination. Both contamination and septic tanks are mentioned in the first sentence. Therefore, the second sentence expands on the first.

17. C: The first sentence states that the Richter Scale is the most commonly-used method to measure the strength of earthquakes. The second sentence states that other methods are used more frequently. Therefore, the second sentence contradicts the information in the first.

18. B: The first sentence introduces the concept of adaptation, which refers to an animal's ability to change in order to increase its chances of survival. A porcupine's quills allow it to defend itself against potential predators, thereby increasing its chances of survival. The second sentence provides an example of the concept presented in the first.

19. D: The first sentence states a problem: congestion due to excessive traffic. The second sentence offers a solution: carpooling can reduce the amount of traffic on roads, which could logically help ease congestion.

20. C: The first sentence describes how men make decisions. The second sentence describes the different process that is used by women to make decisions, which provides a contrast to the first.

Arithmetic Test

1. C: When the numerator and denominator of a fraction are divided or multiplied by the same number, the quotient or product is equivalent to the original fraction. In this case, the numerator and denominator of 6/12 can be divided by two, giving 3/6.

2. D: $675 \times 7 = 4,725$

3. C: $5,465 + 394 = 5,859$

This is closest to 6000 (C).

4. C: Multiply 1/6 by 2 to get a common denominator.

$1/6 \times 2 = 2/12$

Then calculate $11/12 - 2/12 = 9/12$

Reduce this fraction by dividing both numerator and denominator by 3.

$(9 \div 3) / (12 \div 3) = 3/4$

5. B: 743 – 87 = 656

6. A: 75 ÷ 16 = 4.6875

Rounded up to the nearest hundredth, the value is 4.69

7. D: 598 × 46 = 27,508

8. B: An easy way to answer this is to convert all of the answer choices to decimals (which can be done by dividing the numerators by the denominators):

$$1/4 = 0.25$$
$$1/3 = 0.33$$
$$1/2 = 0.5$$
$$3/5 = 0.6$$

1/3 is the closest to 0.35

9. C: 6.52 + 0.2 + 0.05 = 6.77

10. D: Simply divide the numerator by the denominator to convert the fraction into a decimal.

9 ÷ 5 = 1.8

11. B: 0.058 ÷ 6.37 = 0.009

12. C: Numbers that are fewer places to the right of the decimal point are larger. Since A and B have two zeros and the others have one, they can be eliminated. Since C and D have only one zero, the larger value can be determined by simply looking at the values and ignoring the zeros. 7 is a larger value than 6, so 0.072 represents the largest value.

13. A: First, calculate 12% of 56.

56 × 0.12 = 6.72

Then, add this value (the increase) to the original value of 56.

56 + 6.72 = 62.72

Rounding off, we get 62.7

14. B: We know that the factory produces 12 tonnes of cereal per day. Therefore, to calculate how many days it would take to produce 596 tonnes of cereal, divide 596 by 12.

596 ÷ 12 = 49.67

The factory will need most of the fiftieth day to complete the order.

15. B: One side of a square is 56cm. All of its sides are equal, and the perimeter is the sum of all sides.

Therefore, the perimeter equals 56cm+56cm+56cm+56cm

The perimeter is 224cm.

16. A: There are three fractions: 1/4, 1/8, and 1/2.

To answer the question, they have to be added. The common denominator is 8.

2/8 + 1/8 + 4/8 = 7/8

Among just the first three people, the dog is being taken care of 7/8 of the time.

Now, the time that is left over must be calculated.

Using the common denominator of 8, we know that 1 = 8/8

Therefore, to calculate the proportion of time the fourth person will have to care for the dog:

8/8 – 7/8 = 1/8

17. D: Explanation: First, calculate 3% of 548 meters.

548 meters × 0.03 = 16.44 meters.

Then, add it to the original height.

548 meters + 16.44 meters = 564.44 meters

Rounding off, we get 564 meters.

Practice Test #2

Sentence Skills

Directions for questions 1–10

Select the best version of the underlined part of the sentence. The first choice is the same as the original sentence. If you think the original sentence is best, choose the first answer.

1. Children who aren't nurtured during infancy are more likely to develop attachment disorders, <u>which can cause persisting and severely problems</u> later in life.

    a. which can cause persisting and severely problems
    b. that can cause persisting and severe problem
    c. they can cause persistent and severe problem
    d. which can cause persistent and severe problems

2. While speed is a measure of how fast an object is moving, velocity measures how fast an object is moving <u>and also indicates in what direction</u> it is traveling.

    a. and also indicates in what direction
    b. and only indicates in which direction
    c. and also indicate in which directions
    d. and only indicated in what direction

3. Many companies are now using social networking sites like Facebook and MySpace <u>to market their service and product.</u>

    a. to market their service and product
    b. to market their services and products
    c. and market their service and products
    d. which market their services and products

4. An autoclave is a tool used mainly in hospitals <u>to sterilizing surgical tools and hypodermic needles</u>.

    a. to sterilizing surgical tools and hypodermic needles
    b. for sterilize surgical tools and hypodermic needles
    c. to sterilize surgical tools and hypodermic needles
    d. for sterilizing the surgical tool and hypodermic needle

5. <u>The bizarre creatures known by electric eels</u> are capable of emitting an incredible 600 volts of electricity.

    a. The bizarre creatures known by electric eels
    b. A bizarre creature known as electric eels
    c. The bizarre creatures known to electric eels
    d. The bizarre creatures known as electric eels

6. <u>A key factor taken into account during city planning is</u> where major services and amenities will be located.

  a. A key factor taken into account during city planning is
  b. Key factors taken into account during city planning is
  c. A key factor taking into account during city planning is
  d. Key factors, taken into accounting during city planning are

7. Jupiter with its numerous moons, and Great Red Spot, has been studied extensively by astronomers.

  a. Jupiter with its numerous moons, and Great Red Spot,
  b. Jupiter with, its numerous moons and Great Red Spot,
  c. Jupiter, with its numerous moons and Great Red Spot,
  d. Jupiter with, its numerous moons, and Great Red Spot,

8. Many gardeners are now making their own backyard compost, which is not only cheap, but also helps to cut down on landfill waste.

  a. which is not only cheap, but also helps to cut down on landfill waste
  b. which is not only cheaper, but also cuts down on landfill's waste
  c. which is, not only cheap, but also, helps to cut down on landfill waste
  d. which is not only done cheaply, but is also cutting down on landfills wastes

9. <u>The growth of the security industry can be large attributable</u> to the fact that people are less trusting of others than they once were.

  a. The growth of the security industry can be large attributable
  b. The growing of the securities industry can be largely attributable
  c. The growth on the security industry can be large attributed
  d. The growth of the security industry can be largely attributed

10. Claude Monet was a famous painter <u>who's well-known painting includes</u> *San Giorgio Maggiore at Dusk* and *The Water Lily Pond.*.

  a. who's well-known painting includes
  b. whose well-known painting including
  c. whose well-known paintings include
  d. who well-known paintings include

Directions for questions 11–20

Rewrite the sentence in your head following the directions given below. Keep in mind that your new sentence should be well written and should have essentially the same meaning as the original sentence.

11. Bats and dolphins use a process known as echolocation, which means they emit and receive frequencies that can help them navigate through the dark night and murky waters, and also allows them to locate food sources like insects or fish.

Rewrite, beginning with

Locating food sources like insects or fish

The next words will be

    a. during which they emit and receive frequencies
    b. is done through a process known as echolocation
    c. helps them navigate through the dark night
    d. is done by bats and dolphins

12. Carbon dating is an accepted method used by archaeologists to figure out the age of artifacts, even though it may not be entirely accurate if samples are contaminated or if the objects to be dated are not extremely old.

Rewrite, beginning with

Even though carbon dating is not always entirely accurate,

The next words will be

    a. it is an accepted method
    b. objects to be dated
    c. to figure out the age
    d. samples are contaminated

13. Chemical changes are sometimes difficult to distinguish from physical changes, but some examples of physical changes, such as melting water, chopped wood, and ripped paper, are very easy to recognize.

Rewrite, beginning with

Melting water, chopped wood, and ripped paper

The next words will be

    a. are sometimes difficult to distinguish
    b. are very easy to recognize
    c. are chemical changes
    d. are some examples of physical changes

14. The theory of repressed memory was developed by Sigmund Freud, and it stated that all people store memories that cannot be accessed during daily life, but can be accessed through hypnotherapy and hypnosis.

Rewrite, beginning with

Developed by Sigmund Freud,

The next words will be

    a.   it stated that all people
    b.   that cannot be accessed
    c.   hypnotherapy and hypnosis
    d.   the theory of repressed memory

15. Romantic poetry is an important genre, and the works are easily distinguished from other types of poetry by a few characteristics, including their focus on nature and the importance that is ascribed to everyday occurrences.

Rewrite, beginning with

A focus on nature and the importance that is ascribed to everyday occurrences

The next words will be

    a.   are easily distinguished
    b.   from other types of poetry
    c.   are a few characteristics
    d.   is an important genre

16. The Sugar Act was implemented in 1764 by England, and it required individuals residing in the colonies of the United States to pay a tax on sugar, as well as on dyes and other goods.

Rewrite, beginning with

Implemented in 1764 by England

The next words will be

    a.   the Sugar Act
    b.   it required individuals
    c.   in the colonies
    d.   on sugar

17. Oil spill, as the phrase suggests, refers to the accidental introduction of oil into environments, and even though it can refer to land spills, the phrase is usually understood to refer to spills in water.

Rewrite, beginning with

Even though the phrase "oil spill" is usually understood to refer to spills in water

The next words will be

    a.   as the name suggests
    b.   it can refer to land spills
    c.   and the introduction of oil
    d.   known as oil spills

18. Radar was first used in 1904, and at that time all it was capable of was determining whether objects were present, but now it can determine the size and shape of an object, among other things, as well.

Rewrite, beginning with

<u>Although once only capable of determining the presence of objects,</u>

The next words will be

    a. radar was first used
    b. among other things
    c. radar can now determine
    d. the size and shape of an object

19. Placebos are often used in drug studies, and the effectiveness of a drug can be determined by measuring whether people with illnesses or diseases show significantly more improvement when they are given a real drug rather than a placebo.

Rewrite, beginning with

<u>By measuring whether people with illnesses show significantly more improvement when given a real drug,</u>

The next words will be

    a. the effectiveness of a drug
    b. placebos can be used in drug studies
    c. it is rather than a placebo
    d. is often used in drug studies

20. Employees value salary and good benefits in a job, but many also consider having an enjoyable job important, so it's difficult to say what the majority of people value most in a career.

Rewrite, beginning with

<u>While many people consider having an enjoyable job important,</u>

The next words will be

    a. it's what the majority of people
    b. it's difficult to say
    c. salary and good benefits
    d. other employees value

Reading Comprehension

Directions for questions 1–10

Read the statement or passage and then choose the best answer to the question. Answer the question based on what is stated or implied in the statement or passage.

1. The Amazon Rainforest is one of the most important ecosystems in the world. However, it is slowly being destroyed. Areas of the rainforest are being cleared for farms and roads, and much of the wood is also being harvested and sold. There are several compelling reasons to protect this area. First, a significant number of pharmaceuticals are made from plants that have been discovered in the rainforest, and it's quite possible there are still important plants that have not yet been discovered. Secondly, the rainforest provides a significant portion of the world's oxygen and also absorbs great amounts of carbon dioxide. Without rainforests, global warming could accelerate.

The main purpose of the passage is

    a. to present the major reasons why the Amazon Rainforest is being destroyed.
    b. to explain why the Amazon Rainforest should be protected.
    c. to argue that rainforest destruction is a major cause of global warming.
    d. to discuss how the rainforest has helped in the development of medications.

2. Howard Gardner was a psychologist best known for developing the theory of multiple intelligences. Basically, the theory states that the idea of general intelligence or overall intelligence is somewhat inaccurate. This is because people often show intelligence in different areas. He argued that there are actually different types of intelligence. One type of intelligence that Gardner identified was interpersonal intelligence. People who possess this type of intelligence relate and interact well with others. Intrapersonal intelligence, on the other hand, implies that people are in touch with their own feelings. They enjoy thinking about theories and developing their own thoughts and ideas. People who have linguistic intelligence learn best by taking notes and reading textbooks. These people usually excel in traditional academic environments, as many academic subjects stress these types of activities. The other types of intelligence are kinesthetic, musical, spatial, and logical/mathematical.

We can conclude from the passage that

    a. Gardner believed that linguistic intelligence was the most desirable type to have.
    b. most people who have a high level of intrapersonal intelligence do well in school.
    c. people who have a high level of interpersonal intelligence work well in groups.
    d. people who have mathematical intelligence would do the best on a standard IQ test.

3. The Internet has made life a whole lot easier for many people, but being online also brings with it very real risks. Hackers can steal personal and financial information. There are several precautions that computer users can take to minimize the level of risk that is involved with being online. One of the most obvious safety precautions is to purchase a good anti-virus and anti-spyware program. Passwords are also a very important part of online security, and several tips can help users create more secure passwords. First, they should be something that can easily be remembered, but they shouldn't be something others can guess easily. Your first or last name, phone number, or the name of your street are all bad choices, as people could learn this information quite easily. Longer passwords are more secure, and those that use a mixture of upper and lower case letters and a combination of letters and numbers are more secure than those that don't. Finally, passwords should be changed often. This can make remembering them more difficult, but the extra effort is worth the added security.

The main purpose of this passage is to

a. discuss the major risks associated with Internet use.
b. talk about the importance of anti-virus programs.
c. outline important considerations for passwords.
d. discuss why certain types of passwords shouldn't be used.

4. When people are conducting research, particularly historical research, they usually rely on primary and secondary sources. Primary sources are the more direct type of information. They are accounts of an event that are produced by individuals who were actually present. Some examples of primary sources include a person's diary entry about an event, an interview with an eyewitness, a newspaper article, or a transcribed conversation. Secondary sources are pieces of information that are constructed through the use of other primary sources. Often, the person who creates the secondary source was not actually present at the event. Secondary sources could include books, research papers, and magazine articles.

From the passage it can be assumed that

a. primary sources are easier to find than secondary sources.
b. primary sources provide more accurate information than secondary sources.
c. secondary sources give more accurate information than primary sources.
d. secondary sources are always used when books or articles are being written.

5. Many people fail to realize just how crucial getting a good night's sleep actually is. It is usually suggested that adults get about seven hours of sleep every night, and younger children should get even more. Sleep has several benefits. First, it is believed to improve memory. This is one reason why it is always preferable to sleep the night before a test rather than stay up for the entire night to review the information. On a related note, sleep also improves concentration and mental alertness. Those who get sufficient sleep are able to concentrate on work tasks better and also react faster when they are driving a car, for example. Finally, people who get enough sleep have better immunity against illness. The reason for this is not fully understood, but researchers believe that an increase in the production of growth hormone and melatonin plays a role.

The main purpose of this passage is

a. to talk about the benefits of sleep.
b. to discuss how much sleep people should get.
c. to identify which hormones can boost immunity.
d. to present strategies for improving memory and concentration.

6. **Feudalism was a type of social system that existed in parts of Europe during the Middle Ages. Essentially, there were several different classes within a feudal society. The king controlled all of the land in his jurisdiction. He divided this land among a few barons. The barons then divided up the land they were given and distributed it to knights. It was then split up again and distributed to serfs, who were the lowest members of feudal society. They were permitted to farm a small section of land, but they had to give a portion of their food to the knights in exchange for this privilege. They also had to give free labor to the knights who allowed them to use their land. Serfs had very few rights; they weren't even allowed to leave their land without permission from the knight who controlled the land. The system of feudalism ended when money began to be used as currency instead of land.**

It can be concluded that

    a.   serfs were in a better position when the economy changed to a money-based one.

    b.   there were more knights in a typical feudal society than barons.

    c.   the knights did not have to do anything for the barons in exchange for land.

    d.   most feudal societies in Europe were ruled by more than one king.

7. **A bird's feathers are extremely important, and when they clean and smooth them, it is known as preening. Birds in the wild preen their feathers on a regular basis. This is true of most captive birds as well, but not all. For example, some birds do not preen their feathers at all. This problem is most common in birds that are taken from their mothers at a very young age. Presumably, the absence of preening is due to the fact that they were never shown how to do it properly. A more common problem among captive birds is excessive preening. Some birds may pull out large numbers of their feathers or bite them down to the skin. It should be noted that wild birds never exhibit this kind of behavior. There are several suggestions about how the problem of excessive preening can be solved. Giving birds baths or placing them in an area that has more activity to prevent boredom are suggestions. However, these measures are often not sufficient to solve the problem.**

The purpose of the passage is

    a.   to give an overview of abnormal preening in birds.

    b.   to compare captive birds to wild birds.

    c.   to discuss why preening is important.

    d.   to explain how excessive preening problems can be solved.

8. **Hibernation in animals is an extremely fascinating phenomenon, one that biologists are not yet close to understanding fully. However, it is quite easy to understand why animals hibernate during the cold winter months. Usually, it is because their food is quite scarce during this time. Animals that are herbivores will find the winters extremely tough, because all of the vegetation will have died off by the time winter arrives. Hibernation is essentially a way of dealing with this food shortage. Animals like birds rely on seeds and small insects for sustenance. Obviously, these will also be quite scarce in the winter when the ground becomes covered and frozen. Many birds address their upcoming food shortage in quite a different way: they migrate to warmer areas where their sources of food will be plentiful.**

The main reason animals hibernate is

    a.   to travel to a warmer area where food will be more plentiful.

    b.   to cut down on their food consumption during the winter months.

    c.   to avoid the harsh weather that occurs during the winter months.

    d.   to avoid food shortages that occur during the winter months.

9. At one time, the use of leeches to treat medical problems was quite common. If a person suffered from a snake bite or a bee sting, leeches were believed to be capable of removing the poison from the body if they were placed on top of the wound. They have also been used for bloodletting and to stop hemorrhages, although neither of these leech treatments would be considered acceptable by present-day physicians. Today, leeches are still used on a limited basis. Most often, leeches are used to drain blood from clogged veins. This results in little pain for the patient and also ensures the patient's blood will not clot while it is being drained.

The main purpose of the passage is

- a. to discuss the benefits of using leeches to treat blocked veins.
- b. to give an overview of how leeches have been used throughout history.
- c. to compare which uses of leeches are effective and which are not.
- d. to explain how leeches can be used to remove poison from the body.

10. When online file-sharing programs emerged, the music industry changed forever. Perhaps the first widely-used music file sharing program was Napster. It allowed users to sign up to use the service at no charge. Then, they could download music files from other users all over the world by simply typing in what song or album they wanted. Obviously, this was bad news for music artists and record labels because they weren't making any profits from downloaded music. Eventually, Napster was shut down. While it later reinvented itself as a paying service, other free music-sharing sites cropped up almost immediately. Even though several sites and individual users have been charged, there are still countless individuals who log onto these sites to obtain free music.

The main problem associated with peer file-sharing sites is

- a. it is hard to locate users to criminally charge them.
- b. there are too many of them currently in existence.
- c. they prevent artists and labels from earning money.
- d. they allow users to sign up for the service free of charge.

Directions for questions 11–20

For the questions that follow, two underlined sentences are followed by a question or statement. Read the sentences, then choose the best answer to the question or the best completion of the statement.

11. Zoos are places that serve no other purpose than to allow greedy owners to make money. **Some of the world's most endangered animals can be found in zoos, where they are protected from poachers and predators.**

What does the second sentence do?

- a. It challenges the first.
- b. It provides an example.
- c. It supports the first.
- d. It restates the first.

12. Elephants are highly intelligent animals that are known to display several human-like behaviors.

> **When a member of their herd dies, elephants create graves for their fallen comrades, and have been known to visit burial sites years after the elephant's death.**

What does the second sentence do?
   a. It provides a contrast.
   b. It provides an example.
   c. It restates the information from the first.
   d. It offers a solution.

13. Aerobic exercises, which include biking and running, offer several benefits, including better cardiovascular health.

> **Those who regularly walk or do other forms of aerobic exercise typically have a lower resting heart rate and suffer fewer heart problems.**

What does the second sentence do?
   a. It offers a solution.
   b. It presents an example.
   c. It contradicts the information in the first.
   d. It expands on the information in the first.

14. Despite advancements in contraceptive technologies, teen pregnancy is still a huge problem in the United States.

> **Many schools are choosing not to teach students about contraception, and that means many may not be aware of how to obtain effective contraceptives.**

What does the second sentence do?
   a. It expands on the information in the first.
   b. It offers a solution.
   c. It provides an explanation.
   d. It restates the information in the first.

15. Although it may seem impossible, solving a Rubik's Cube is quite doable if one knows about the various solving methods.

> **Manipulating the cube so that all of the corner pieces are in their correct positions and then essentially filling in the blanks is a time-consuming but effective solving method.**

What does the second sentence do?
   a. It contrasts with the first.
   b. It offers an explanation.
   c. It restates the information in the first.
   d. It expands on the information in the first.

16. Many people now use digital devices such as PDAs to keep track of their schedules.

> **PDAs are easy to use and, unlike day planners, there is no need to carry around a bulky notebook or search for a pen when you need to add something.**

How are the sentences related?
- a. They provide a statement and an explanation.
- b. They present a problem and a possible solution.
- c. They present a principle and an example.
- d. They contradict each other.

17. DDT is a pesticide that is thought to adversely affect bird populations and contribute to the incidence of cancer in humans.

> **In 1972, the use of DDT in the United States was banned.**

What does the second sentence do?
- a. It supports the first.
- b. It states a result.
- c. It gives an example.
- d. It provides an explanation.

18. People who are concerned about the very real and sometimes serious side effects of conventional drugs are now turning to natural remedies.

> **Natural remedies offer an alternative to drugs prescribed by doctors, which can often have serious adverse effects.**

How are the two sentences related?
- a. They contradict each other.
- b. They support each other.
- c. They repeat the same information.
- d. They present a cause and an effect.

19. Students should study what they are passionate about when they attend university.

> **Any individual considering university should research the job market and make decisions about what they will study based on current employment trends.**

What does the second sentence do?
- a. It contradicts the first.
- b. It provides an example.
- c. It expands on the first.
- d. It offers a solution.

20. Biological weapons, although considered by many to be relatively new, have actually been used by militaries for thousands of years.

> **In Greece, one military used biological warfare by throwing venomous snakes onto the ship of their enemy.**

What does the second sentence do?
- a. It offers a solution.
- b. It provides an example.
- c. It contradicts the first.
- d. It presents an effect.

Arithmetic Test

Solve the following problems and select your answer from the choices given. You may use the paper you have been given for scratch paper.

1. 9/81 is equivalent to which fraction?

    a. 1/18
    b. 1/9
    c. 3/9
    d. 5/9

2. 2 3/4 + 12 6/8 =

    a. 14 1/2
    b. 14 3/4
    c. 15 3/8
    d. 15 1/2

3. 789 – 32 =

    a. 737
    b. 747
    c. 757
    d. 767

4. 56 × 96 is closest to which value?

    a. 5,300
    b. 5,400
    c. 5,500
    d. 5,600

5. 456 / 23 =

    a. 19.83
    b. 19.93
    c. 20.03
    d. 20.63

6. 6/12 + 6/24 + 1/4 =

    a. 1/2
    b. 3/4
    c. 1
    d. 1 1/2

7. Which value is closest to 85% of 25?

    a. 16
    b. 18
    c. 20
    d. 22

8. 0.98 / 0.54 =

    a. 0.181

    b. 1.81

    c. 18.1

    d. 181

9. 1.45 × 0.99 =

    a. 1.44

    b. 2.44

    c. 3.44

    d. 4.44

10. 2.45 + 0.54 + 0.07 =

    a. 2.07

    b. 2.47

    c. 2.97

    d. 3.06

11. Which of the following represents the smallest value?

    a. 0.0009

    b. 0.00095

    c. 0.00089

    d. 0.000799

12. 5.36 - 0.78 =

    a. 4.38

    b. 4.58

    c. 5.37

    d. 5.48

13. Janet makes homemade dolls. Currently, she produces 23 dolls per month. If she increased her production by 18%, how many dolls would Janet produce each month?

    a. 27

    b. 32

    c. 38

    d. 40

14. Two cars are side by side. One is 3.9 meters long. The other is 6% shorter. How long is the second car? Round to the nearest tenth.

    a. 3.5 meters

    b. 3.7 meters

    c. 3.9 meters

    d. 4.1 meters

15. A rectangle's width is 23 cm and its length is 9 cm. What is its area?

    a. 32 cm²

    b. 104 cm²

    c. 207cm²

    d. 311 cm²

16. Three children decide to buy a gift for their father. The gift costs $78.00. One child contributes $24.00. The second contributes $15.00 less than the first. How much will the third child have to contribute?

    a. $15.00
    b. $39.00
    c. $45.00
    d. $62.00

17. Bruce is attending a conference that is 827 km from his home. If he travels at a speed of 64km/hour, approximately how long will it take him to reach his destination?

    a. 5 hours
    b. 9 hours
    c. 13 hours
    d. 17 hours

Answer Key and Explanations

Sentence Skills

1. D: Answer choice A is incorrect because *severely* is an adverb and not an adjective. B and C are incorrect because *problem* instead of the grammatically correct *problems* is used. D uses the correct, plural form *problems* and uses adjectives to describe the problems.

2. A: The sentence implies that *velocity* is used to indicate more than one value, which eliminates B and D. The phrase refers to velocity, which is singular, but the construction of choice C would correctly refer to a plural noun. Choice A agrees with the singular, noun and the *and* indicates that velocity is used to indicate more than one value.

3. B: Answer choice B uses the grammatically correct *their* instead of *there*. The *to* indicates the companies are using these sites for something, and *services* and *products* agree with each other because they are both plural.

4. C: Answer choice C states that an autoclave is a tool used *to sterilize*. A and B, which begin with *to sterilizing* and *for sterilize*, are not grammatically correct. D indicates that the machine is used to sterilize a single tool and needle, which does not make sense in the context of the sentence.

5. D: Answer choices A and C are incorrect because they imply that the bizarre creatures are something other than electric eels. The *a* in choice B does not agree with the plural *electric eels*. Choice D is best because it is grammatically correct and identifies electric eels as the bizarre creatures being discussed in the sentence.

6. A: Answer choice B is incorrect because the plural *key factors* and the singular *is* do not agree. The *taking* in choice C makes it incorrect. Choice D has a misplaced comma. Choice A makes sense and the singular *a key factor* and *is* agree with each other.

7. C: Choice C is the only choice that has correctly placed commas. The *numerous moons* and the *Great Red Spot* both refer to the planet Jupiter, which is maintained in answer choice C.

8. A: Answer choice B is incorrect because of the misplaced apostrophe. C has two unnecessary commas. Answer choice D is too wordy, and *landfills wastes* sounds quite awkward. Answer choice A is succinct, the comma is in the correct place, and it expresses the information is a clear way that is not awkward.

9. D: Answer choices A and C are incorrect because *large* is used in front of *attributable* and *attributed*. Both of these phrases are grammatically incorrect. B describes *the growing of the securities industry*, which is quite awkward. D is the best choice because it refers to *the growth of the security industry* and uses the phrase *largely attributed*, which is grammatically correct.

10. C: The correct way to refer to a person, in this case Monet, is through the use of the pronoun *whose*, which eliminates A and D. Two paintings are identified, so the plural form must be used, eliminating choice B. Choice C uses *whose* and *paintings*, indicating there is more than one, making it the correct choice.

11. B: The original sentence indicates that bats and dolphins are able to do many things, including locating food sources like insects or fish through a process known as echolocation. Answer choice B best expresses the fact that locating food is accomplished through echolocation. Answer choice C

cannot logically follow the phrase. Answer choices A and D do not tell how bats and dolphins locate food.

12. A: The new sentence begins with the phrase "even though," indicating that a contrast is being constructed. "Even though carbon dating is not always entirely accurate, it is still an accepted method" provides this contrast, while the other choices do not.

13. D: Melting water, chopped wood, and ripped paper are identified in the original sentence as examples of physical changes that are easy to distinguish from chemical changes. Therefore, answer choices A and C are entirely incorrect. Answer choice B indicates that these objects are easy to recognize, but the sentence should convey that they are examples of physical changes that are easy to recognize, making this choice somewhat inaccurate. Choice D is best because it identifies the previously mentioned objects as examples of physical changes.

14. D: The only phrase that describes something developed by Sigmund Freud is D. Answer choice A does not identify what the *it* is referring to, and B cannot logically follow the given phrase. Answer choice C describes ways to access repressed memories, but these were not developed by Freud.

15. C: A focus on nature and ascribing importance to everyday occurrences are identified in the original sentence as important characteristics of Romantic poetry. Answer choice C clearly identifies them as characteristics, and is the only choice that can logically follow the given phrase.

16. A: The Sugar Act is identified in the first sentence as something that was implemented in 1764 by England. Therefore, answer choice A is the best choice. Answer choice B does not indicate what was implemented. Answer choice C indicates where but not what was implemented, and D does not tell the reader what was implemented.

17. B: The phrase "even though" indicates a contrast. Answer choice A is more of an agreement than a contrast. Answer choice C is somewhat redundant, and D cannot logically follow the given phrase. Answer choice B provides a contrast because the given phrase talks about spills in water, while choice B talks about spills on land. It is also a logical choice because "it" in choice B refers to "the phrase" that is mentioned in the given phrase.

18. C: C is the only choice that provides a distinction between then and now. The given phrase says that radar was *once* used to determine the presence of objects, and C indicates that radar can *now* determine other things as well.

19. A: The word "by" indicates a cause/effect relationship. By measuring whether people respond significantly more favorably when given a real drug, something is being accomplished. Answer choices C and D do not imply this relationship. Answer choice B does not make logical sense in the context of the sentence. Answer choice A states "the effectiveness of a drug," which is a good choice because it could logically be followed with a phrase like "can be determined."

20. D: The word "while" is used to establish a contrast, making D the obvious choice. The given phrase speaks about *some people*, while D identifies *other employees*, which creates an effective contrast.

Reading Comprehension

1. B: Answer choices A and C are mentioned only briefly. D is discussed, but it falls under the more general purpose of the passage, which is discussing why the Amazon Rainforest is a valuable area that should be protected.

2. C: Answer choice A is not a logical conclusion because there is no indication that Gardner ranked the intelligences in any way. Answer choice B cannot be concluded from the passage, as there is no mention of the value placed on intrapersonal intelligences in a traditional academic environment. IQ tests are not mentioned at all, so we cannot conclude anything about them based on this passage. Answer choice C is the correct choice. Those with interpersonal intelligence interact well with others, so it is reasonable to assume they would perform well in a group setting.

3. C: Answer choices A and B are touched upon only very briefly. Answer choice D is discussed, but it is encompassed by the broader purpose of the passage, which is to outline the most important considerations related to passwords.

4. B: Answer choice B is the most logical conclusion. The passage states that, "Primary sources are the more direct type of information. They are accounts of an event that are produced by individuals who were actually present." Therefore, it is reasonable to assume that an account prepared by someone who was present would be more accurate than one prepared by somebody decades later who had to rely on the accounts of others.

5. A: Answer choices B and C are mentioned only briefly, and D is not really discussed in the passage. The passage focuses mainly on discussing some of the major benefits of sleep, so that is the main purpose of the passage.

6. B: Answer choice B is the logical conclusion. The passage states that "The king controlled all of the land in his jurisdiction. He divided this among a few barons. The barons then divided up the land they were given and distributed it to knights." If the barons divided up their lands, it would stand to reason that each baron would distribute his land to several knights. Therefore, there would have to be more knights than barons.

7. A: Answer choice B is not correct, because wild birds are not discussed at length. Answer choice C is not really discussed, and D is touched upon only briefly. The passage focuses on lack of preening and excessive preening, which are both examples of abnormal preening behavior. The main purpose of the passage is to discuss abnormal preening in birds.

8. D: The passage states that "Animals that are herbivores will find the winters extremely tough, because all of the vegetation will have died off by the time winter arrives. Hibernation is essentially a way of dealing with this food shortage." Therefore, D is the correct answer. Answer choice A is the purpose of migration, and answer choices B and C are not mentioned.

9. B: Answer choices A, C, and D are all mentioned in the passage, but they are part of the overall purpose, which is to give an overview of how leeches have been used throughout history.

10. C: The passage states that "Obviously, this was bad news for music artists and record labels because they weren't making any profits from downloaded music." Therefore, answer choice C is the correct choice. None of the other choices are identified as problems associated with file-sharing sites.

11. A: The first sentence states that the only purpose of zoos is to allow greedy people to profit. The second sentence challenges the first, however, pointing out that a key purpose of zoos is to protect endangered animals.

12. B: The first sentence states that elephants are capable of human-like behaviors. The second sentence states that elephants bury their dead and visit graves, which provides examples of human-like behaviors.

13. D: The first sentence mentions that cardiovascular health is a benefit of aerobic exercise. The second sentence mentions low resting heart rates and fewer cardiovascular problems, which are signs of good cardiovascular health. Therefore, the second sentence expands on the information in the first.

14. C: The first sentence identifies a problem: persisting high rates of teen pregnancy in spite of advancements in contraceptive technology. The second sentence offers a possible explanation: young people aren't being informed about how they can access contraceptives.

15. D: The first sentence mentions that various solutions for solving a Rubik's cube exist. The second sentence explains one in greater detail. Therefore, the second sentence expands on the information in the first.

16. A: The first sentence states that many people use digital devices to keep track of their schedules. The second describes several key advantages of PDAs that could possibly explain their popularity. Therefore, the sentences provide a statement and an explanation.

17. B: The first sentence states that DDT is a substance believed to be harmful to people and wildlife. The second sentence states that its use was banned in the United States. This ban is a direct result of the discovery of the harm that DDT can cause.

18. C: The two sentences express the same idea, and no new information is added in the second sentence. Therefore, the two sentences repeat the same information.

19. A: The first sentence states students should make decisions about what they will study in university based on their interests. The second states they should make decisions based on the job market. The second sentence directly contradicts the first.

20. B: The first sentence states that biological weapons have been used by militaries for many years. The second sentence tells about an army that threw poisonous snakes onto the ships of their enemies. The second sentence provides an example of biological weapons that were used long ago.

Arithmetic Test

1. B: When the numerator and denominator of a fraction are divided or multiplied by the same number, the product is an equivalent fraction. In this case, the numerator and denominator of 9/81 can be divided by nine, giving 1/9.

2. D: 2 3/4 + 12 6/8 =

First, ensure both fractions have a common denominator:

2 6/8 + 12 6/8 =

14 12/8

12/8 is greater than one, so express it as a whole number and a fraction: 1 4/8

Add this value to 14.

14 + 1 4/8 =

15 4/8

Reduce 4/8 by dividing the numerator and denominator by 4.

15 1/2

3. C: 789 – 32 = 757

4. B: 56 × 96 = 5376

This value is closest to 5400.

5. A: 456 ÷ 23 = 19.826

Rounding up, we get 19.83

6. C: 6/12 + 6/24 + 1/4 =

The common denominator is 24.

12/24 + 6/24 + 6/24 = 24/24

= 1

7. D: First, calculate 85% of 25.

25 x 0.85 = 21.25

This value is closest to 22 (D).

8. B: 0.98 / 0.54 = 1.81

9. A: 1.45 × .99 = 1.4355

Rounding up, we get 1.44

10. D: 2.45 + 0.54 + 0.07 = 3.06

11. D: Numbers that are farther to the right of the decimal point are smaller. Since all of the numbers have three zeros in front of them (that is, they are in the ten-thousandths place), look at the first number that is not a zero. The smallest number will represent the smallest value. Since the first number in D is 7, the lowest number, D represents the lowest value.

12. B: 5.36 - 0.78 = 4.58

13. A: First, calculate 18% of 23.

23 × 0.18 = 4.14

Then, add this value (the increase) to the original value of 23.

23 + 4.14 = 27.14

Rounding off, we get 27.

14. B: First, calculate 6% of 3.9.

3.9 × 0.06 = 0.234

Then, subtract this value (the decrease) from the original value of 3.9.

3.9 – 0.234 = 3.666 meters

Rounding off, we get 3.7 meters

15. C: The formula for the area of a rectangle is length × width.

Therefore,

$$A = l \times w$$
$$A = 9cm \times 23cm$$
$$A = 207cm2$$

16. C: First, figure out how much the second child contributed:

$$\$24.00 - \$15.00 = \$9.00$$

Then, calculate how much the first two children contributed in total:

$$\$24.00 + \$9.00 = \$33.00$$

Finally, figure out how much the third child will have to contribute:

$$\$78.00 - \$33.00 = \$45.00$$

17. C: The distance that is being traveled and the speed are known. To find the time, simply set up these values in the following way.

827 ~~km~~ x <u>1 hour</u> = x (the number of hours the trip will take)

      64 ~~km~~

827/64 = 12.92 hours

Rounding off, we get 13 hours.

Practice Test #3

Sentence Skills

Directions for questions 1–10

Select the best version of the underlined part of the sentence. The first choice is the same as the original sentence. If you think the original sentence is best, choose the first answer.

1. If he stops to consider the ramifications of this decision, it is probable that he will rethink his original decision a while longer.

- a.   it is probable that he will rethink his original decision.
- b.   he will rethink his original decision over again.
- c.   he probably will rethink his original decision.
- d.   he will most likely rethink his original decision for a bit.

2. When you get older," she said "you will no doubt understand what I mean."

- a.   older," she said "you will no doubt
- b.   older" she said "you will no doubt
- c.   older," she said, "you will no doubt
- d.   older," she said "you will not

3. Dr. Anderson strolled past the nurses, examining a bottle of pills.

- a.   Dr. Anderson strolled past the nurses, examining a bottle of pills.
- b.   Dr. Anderson strolled past the nurses examining a bottle of pills.
- c.   Examining a bottle of pills Dr. Anderson strolled past the nurses.
- d.   Examining a bottle of pills, Dr. Anderson strolled past the nurses.

4. Karl and Henry raced to the reservoir, climbed the ladder, and then they dove into the cool water.

- a.   raced to the reservoir, climbed the ladder, and then they dove into
- b.   first raced to the reservoir, climbed the ladder, and then they dove into
- c.   raced to the reservoir, they climbed the ladder, and then they dove into
- d.   raced to the reservoir, climbed the ladder, and dove into

5. Did either Tracy or Vanessa realize that her decision would be so momentous?

- a.   Tracy or Vanessa realize that her decision would be
- b.   Tracy or Vanessa realize that each of their decision was
- c.   Tracy or Vanessa realize that her or her decision would be
- d.   Tracy or Vanessa realize that their decision would be

6. Despite their lucky escape, Jason and his brother could not hardly enjoy themselves.

- a.   Jason and his brother could not hardly enjoy themselves.
- b.   Jason and his brother could not enjoy themselves.
- c.   Jason and Jason's brother could not hardly enjoy themselves.
- d.   Jason and his brother could not enjoy them.

71

7. Stew recipes call for rosemary, parsley, thyme, and these sort of herbs.

    a. for rosemary, parsley, thyme, and these sort of herbs.
    b. for: rosemary; parsley; thyme; and these sort of herbs.
    c. for rosemary, parsley, thyme, and these sorts of herbs.
    d. for rosemary, parsley, thyme, and this sorts of herbs.

8. Mr. King, an individual of considerable influence, created a personal fortune and gave back to the community.

    a. an individual of considerable influence, created a personal fortune and gave back
    b. an individual of considerable influence, he created a personal fortune and gave back
    c. an individual of considerable influence created a personal fortune and gave back
    d. an individual of considerable influence, created a personal fortune and gave it back

9. She is the person whose opinion matters the most.

    a. She is the person whose opinion matters the most.
    b. She is the person to whom opinion matters the most.
    c. She is the person who matters the most, in my opinion.
    d. She is the person for whom opinion matters the most.

10. Minerals are nutritionally significant elements <u>that assist to make your body</u> work properly.

    a. that assist to make your body
    b. that help your body
    c. that making your body
    d. that work to make your body

Directions for questions 11–20

Rewrite the sentence in your head following the directions given below. Keep in mind that your new sentence should be well written and should have essentially the same meaning as the original sentence.

11. The Burmese python is a large species of snake that is native to parts of southern Asia, although the snake has recently begun infesting the Florida Everglades and causing environmental concerns by devouring endangered species.

Rewrite, beginning with

> <u>The Burmese python has recently caused environmental concerns in the Florida Everglades</u>.

The words that follow will be

    a. because it is devouring endangered species in Florida
    b. where it has made a home for itself away from its origins in southern Asia
    c. by leaving its native home of southern Asia with an infestation of its natural prey
    d. and is altering the delicate balance of species in that area

12. In the wild, the Burmese python typically grows to around twelve feet in length, but in captivity the snakes can often grow much longer than that, to upwards of fifteen or twenty feet in length.

Rewrite, beginning with

<u>Burmese pythons in captivity can grow to be as long as fifteen or twenty feet.</u>

The words that follow will be

   a. as a result of the controlled environment that allows them to eat more
   b. while it is typically shorter in the wild
   c. but in the wild are shorter and may only be twelve feet long
   d. which is much longer than a python in the wild grows to be

13. Florida biologists and environmentalists blame the exotic animals industry for the snake's introduction into the Everglades, because many snake owners are unable or unwilling to continue taking care of the creature once it grows too large and becomes too expensive.

Rewrite, beginning with

<u>*The Burmese python can grow large and become too expensive for snake owners to maintain.*</u>

The words that follow will be

   a. and Florida biologists and environmentalists blame the exotic animals industry
   b. so the python has been introduced into the Everglades
   c. leaving the exotic animals industry at risk in the United States
   d. resulting in abandoned snakes that have infested the Everglades

14. Lawmakers called for action against owning Burmese pythons after a pet python got out of its cage in a Florida home and killed a young child while she was sleeping, a situation that left responsible snake owners objecting and claiming that this was an isolated event.

Rewrite, beginning with

<u>*Responsible Burmese python owners have claimed that the death of a young child in Florida after a python attack was an isolated event.*</u>

The words that follow will be

   a. but lawmakers have called for action against owning the pythons
   b. because the python accidentally got out of its cage and attacked the child
   c. that does not reflect accurately on conscientious snake owners
   d. resulting in angry lawmakers who called for a prohibition of Burmese pythons

15. Biologists were initially concerned that the Burmese python could spread throughout much of the United States, due to its ability to adapt to its environment, but recent evidence suggests that the snake is content to remain within the Everglades.

Rewrite, beginning with

<u>*Recent evidence suggests that the Burmese python is content to remain within the Everglades.*</u>

The words that follow will be

   a. due to its ability to adapt to its environment
   b. and comes as a surprise to biologists who believed the snake would spread outside Florida
   c. despite concerns that the snake could spread throughout much of the United States
   d. because it is unable to adapt to cooler environments outside of south Florida

16. The most prolific predator in the Florida Everglades has always been the alligator, which preys on local birds and wildlife, while the introduction of the Burmese python adds another, and often insatiable, predator to compete with the alligator.

Rewrite, beginning with

> The introduction of the Burmese python to the Everglades adds another predator to compete with the alligator.

The words that follow will be

a. which has always been the most prolific predator in the Everglades
b. thus leaving the local birds and wildlife in serious danger of becoming endangered
c. and the alligator was never as serious a predator as the python has become
d. which does not have the python's reputation for being insatiable

17. Not only does the Burmese python compete with the alligator for prey, but it also competes with the alligator as prey, because pythons have been known to engorge full-grown alligators, thus placing the python at the top of the food chain and leaving them with no native predators in the Everglades.

Rewrite, beginning with

> The Burmese python is now at the top of the food chain in the Everglades and has no native predator.

The words that follow will be

a. so it competes with the alligator as prey
b. as evidence shows that pythons are capable of engorging full-grown alligators
c. although the python still competes with alligators for prey
d. leaving the Everglades with a serious imbalance of predators

18. Biologists and environmentalists recognize the considerable dangers of the python's expansion in the Everglades as it consumes endangered creatures native to that area, and in one instance researchers were shocked to discover that the tracking device for a tagged rodent led them to the python who had already consumed the unlucky creature.

Rewrite, beginning with

> Researchers in the Everglades were shocked to discover that the tracking device for a tagged rodent led them to the python who had already consumed the unlucky creature.

The words that follow will be

a. thus showing how the python is destroying endangered species within the Everglades
b. causing concerns that the python expansion might be more dangerous than biologists and environmentalists originally believed
c. which was one of the few of its species that had managed to survive the python expansion in the Everglades
d. leaving biologists and environmentalists to recognize the considerable dangers of the python's expansion in the Everglades

19. In an attempt at controlling the python, Florida dispatched hunters to destroy as many pythons as possible, but after several months of searching the hunters were only able to make a dent in the python population of thousands by killing several dozen.

Rewrite, beginning with

The python population of thousands was reduced only by several dozen.

The words that follow will be

    a. even after many months of searching for and destroying the creatures
    b. because the hunters were only given a few months for the task and needed more time to destroy as many pythons as possible
    c. after the hunters sent to destroy as many pythons as possible failed to make a dent in the number
    d. resulting in concerns that more hunters were needed to locate and destroy as many pythons as possible

20. Although eradication is preferred when non-native species are introduced into the United States, researchers have found that is it virtually impossible, and controlling the species becomes the only real option in avoiding the destruction of native habitats and endangered species.

Rewrite, beginning with

Controlling an invasive species is the only real option in avoiding the destruction of native habitats and endangered species.

The words that follow will be

    a. because the total eradication of non-native species that are introduced into the United States is virtually impossible
    b. because the total eradication of non-native species that are introduced into the United States is generally frowned upon
    c. although researchers prefer the total eradication of non-native species and continue to make efforts to destroy the python in the Everglades
    d. in spite of the many attempts at totally eradicating the non-native species that are introduced into the United States

Reading Comprehension

Directions for questions 1–10

Read the statement or passage and then choose the best answer to the question. Answer the question based on what is stated or implied in the statement or passage.

1. The so-called anti-aging industry is worth a staggering amount of money in North America. Women are sold all sorts of creams and ointments and are promised that these will make them look younger over time. Unfortunately, these claims are entirely false. Lotions cannot penetrate to the inner layers of the skin where wrinkles typically form. Therefore, no over-the-counter creams are effective at erasing lines and wrinkles.

According to the author, the anti-aging industry

    a. targets its products at men and women equally.
    b. sells products that are highly effective.
    c. is still a relatively small industry.
    d. sells goods that do not do what they promise.

2. There is a clear formula that many students are taught when it comes to writing essays. The first is to develop an introduction, which outlines what will be discussed in the work. It also includes the thesis statement. Next comes the supporting paragraphs. Each paragraph contains a topic sentence, supporting evidence, and finally a type of mini-conclusion that restates the point of the paragraph. Finally, the conclusion sums up the purpose of the paper and emphasizes that the thesis statement was proven.

After the topic sentence,

    a. a thesis statement is included.
    b. supporting evidence is presented.
    c. the conclusion is stated.
    d. the author outlines what will be discussed.

3. The importance of a comfortable work space cannot be overstated. Developing a comfortable work environment is relatively simple for employers. Ergonomic chairs, large computer screens, personal desk space, and some level of privacy are all essential. This involves some expense, but not a great deal. Not surprisingly, employees are happier in this type of environment, but it is the employers who really benefit. Reduced sick time, higher levels of employee satisfaction, higher productivity, and more creativity have all been observed.

The main idea expressed in this passage is

    a. a comfortable work space is not as important as people say.
    b. developing a comfortable work space is easy.
    c. establishing a comfortable work space is not expensive.
    d. employers benefit greatly when they provide comfortable work spaces.

4. Planning weddings is tough. One important part of the planning process is choosing bridesmaid dresses. Although there used to be a lot of rules when it came to picking out a color, many of them are not observed any more. However, one that is still observed is that the bridesmaids should not wear the same color as the bride. The most popular colors for bridesmaid dresses in recent years have been white and black.

It can be concluded that

    a. picking dresses is the hardest part of planning a wedding.
    b. many brides are choosing to wear colors other than white.
    c. most bridesmaids are allowed to choose their own dress.
    d. bridesmaids were not traditionally allowed to wear black.

5. Those so-called green fuels may not be as environmentally friendly as once thought. For example, producing natural gas is a much more labor intensive process than producing an equal amount of conventional gasoline. Also, producing natural gas involves burning fossil fuels. Transporting natural gas also involves burning fossil fuels.

The weakness of green fuels is that

    a. they are not as abundant as conventional fuel.
    b. they require a lot more work to produce.
    c. burning them releases fossil fuels.
    d. they must be transported greater distances.

6. The media has done a lot to promote racism in the United States. For example, it was found that the majority of crimes discussed on the nightly news featured African American suspects. However, when the total number of crimes committed in the US was examined, it was found that white people were also suspects 50% of the time.

If the above information were true, it could be concluded that

    a. there are more white criminals than African American criminals.
    b. most people believe that African Americans commit more crimes.
    c. many crimes committed by white people are not discussed on the news.
    d. the total number of crimes committed has decreased in the last several years.

7. Many people feel that the use of stem cells in research is unethical. However, they fail to realize that such research could lead to cures for some of the world's most troubling diseases. Diseases like Parkinson's and MS could possibly be cured through the use of stem cells, and those with spinal cord injuries could possibly walk again. Therefore, it is entirely ethical to engage in stem cell research aimed at easing the suffering of those who have life-altering conditions.

The main purpose of the passage is

    a. to discuss why people believe stem cell research is unethical.
    b. to discuss the possible benefits of stem cell research.
    c. to identify diseases that have been cured through stem cell research.
    d. to argue that not conducting stem cell research is unethical.

8. Many people do not know the difference between precision and accuracy. While accuracy means that something is correct, precision simply means that you are able to duplicate results and that they are consistent. For example, if there was a glass of liquid that was 100 degrees, an accurate measurement would be one that was close to this temperature. However, if you measured the temperature five times, and came up with a measurement of exactly 50 degrees each time, your measurement would be extremely precise, but not accurate.

The term accurate results refers to

    a. results that are correct.
    b. results that are consistent.
    c. results that can be duplicated.
    d. results that are measurable.

9. Literacy rates are lower today than they were fifteen years ago. Then, most people learned to read through the use of phonics. Today, whole language programs are favored by many educators.

If these statements are true, it can be concluded that

    a. whole language is more effective at teaching people to read than phonics.
    b. phonics is more effective at teaching people to read than whole language.
    c. literacy rates will probably continue to decline over the next 15 years.
    d. the definition of what it means to be literate is much stricter now.

10. George Washington was a remarkable man. He was born in 1732. Shortly before becoming the President of the United States in 1789, Washington was an important leader in the American Revolutionary War from 1775 to 1783. After retiring, he returned to Mount Vernon in 1797. A short time later, John Adams made him commander in chief of the United States Army again. This was done in anticipation that the country might go to war with France.

Almost immediately after serving as a leader in the American Revolutionary War

    a. Washington returned to Mount Vernon.
    b. Washington was made commander in chief of the US Army.
    c. Washington became the President of the United States.
    d. Washington decided to go into retirement.

11. The history of the samurai in Japan is believed to date back to the late 7th century during a period of administrative reform that greatly reorganized Japan. In 663, Japan lost the Battle of Hakusukinoe against the Tang Dynasty of China.

What does the second sentence do?

    a. It undermines the first.
    b. It explains the first.
    c. It restates the first.
    d. It refutes the first.

12. The reform process did not initially create the warrior system that later became the samurai. The bureaucrats known as samurai were administrative officials whose name came from a word that meant "to serve."

What does the second sentence do?

    a. It examines the first.
    b. It reaffirms the first.
    c. It clarifies the first.
    d. It defines a term.

13. During attempts to conquer the island of Honshu, the 8th- and 9th-century Emperor Kammu relied on his serf army to accomplish the task. The emperor used clan members from his aristocracy to succeed in adding Honshu to Japan.

What does the second sentence do?

    a. It explains the first.
    b. It undermines the first.
    c. It offers essential evidence.
    d. It classifies the main idea.

14. The aristocratic clan members represented a powerful force in Emperor Kammu's army, due to their horseback skills and knowledge of weaponry, and he dismissed them following the victory at Honshu. Kammu slowly lost power in the 9th century.

What does the second sentence do?

    a. It presents a new theory.
    b. It transitions to a new idea.
    c. It adds crucial information.
    d. It implies a consequence.

15. The aristocratic clans began establishing their social and political power within Japanese culture. The clan members made powerful marriages, created treaties with other clans, and placed themselves under the code of the Bushido.

What does the second sentence do?

    a. It offers a comparison.
    b. It classifies a system.
    c. It elaborates on an idea.
    d. It refutes the main idea.

16. The Bushido represents an ethical system that shaped the clan leaders into a warrior class, or the samurai. The code of the Bushido encouraged personal honor, the responsibility of the warrior to the lord, and loyalty to the lord even to the point of death.

What does the second sentence do?

    a. It develops the first.
    b. It establishes an effect.
    c. It contrasts with the first.
    d. It establishes the main idea.

17. The samurai grew in political and social authority during the late 12th century and the early 13th century. In 1185, the samurai were successful during their participation in the Battle of Dan-no-Ura.

What does the second sentence do?

    a. It examines the first.
    b. It questions the main idea.
    c. It offers comparative detail.
    d. It suggests a cause.

18. By the end of the 13th century, the samurai grew to be more powerful than the aristocrats they were intended to support. The samurai loyalty to the lord, as required by the Bushido code, became a purely nominal fidelity.

What does the second sentence do?

    a. It undermines the main idea.
    b. It restates the point of the first.
    c. It counters the presented theory.
    d. It examines a supporting thought.

19. Eventually, the samurai were so successful that their warrior services were no longer as necessary as they had been in the past. The samurai began to turn to more artistic pursuits, such as writing poetry and composing music.

What does the second sentence do?

    a. It provides comparative detail.
    b. It establishes an argument.
    c. It elaborates on the main idea.
    d. It offers essential information.

20. Despite a commitment to honorable death, many samurai still feared the prospect of dying by violent means. The principles of Zen Buddhism that were practiced among the samurai included personal discipline, meditation, and self-realization.

What does the second sentence do?

    a. It calls supporting information into question.
    b. It elaborates on a theory presented in the first.
    c. It suggests a cause and effect relationship.
    d. It compares and contrasts two systems of thought.

Arithmetic Test

Solve the following problems and select your answer from the choices given. You may use the paper you have been given for scratch paper.

1. Which number can be divided by 7 with no remainder?

    a. 42
    b. 48
    c. 51
    d. 67

2. Which of the following is equal to 12.5%?

    a. $\dfrac{1}{4}$
    b. $\dfrac{1}{8}$
    c. $\dfrac{1}{12}$
    d. $\dfrac{1}{16}$

3. Which of the following numbers is NOT prime?

    a. 3
    b. 6
    c. 17
    d. 41

4. The number 5 is multiplied by its reciprocal. What is the result?

    a. 0
    b. 1
    c. 1/5
    d. 5

5. Solve: $\dfrac{11}{8} + 7 + \dfrac{3}{4} + \dfrac{4}{3} = 11$?

    a. $12\dfrac{5}{8}$
    b. $11\dfrac{5}{12}$
    c. $12\dfrac{5}{3}$
    d. $10\dfrac{11}{24}$

6. Lauren had $80 in her savings account. When she got her paycheck, she made a deposit that brought the total to $120. By what percentage did the total amount in her account increase as a result of this deposit?

    a. 50%
    b. 40%
    c. 35%
    d. 80%

7. Round 17.188 to the nearest hundredth.

    a. 17.1
    b. 17.2
    c. 17.18
    d. 17.19

8. What number is 3 more than 20% of 70?

    a. 14
    b. 17
    c. 18
    d. 21

9. What number added to 23 makes a number equal to one half of 94?

    a. 21
    b. 23
    c. 24
    d. 26

10. What is the difference between 45 and the average of 20, 35, 45, and 20?

    a. 0
    b. 15
    c. 17
    d. 20

11. A rectangle is twice as long as it is wide. If the width is 3 meters, what is the area in m²?

    a. 12 m2
    b. 6 m2
    c. 9 m2
    d. 18 m2

12. Which number is 300% of the difference between 23 and 27?

    a. 4
    b. 75
    c. 12
    d. 25

13. Which of the following sums is the greatest?

    a. 3 + 4 + 16
    b. 6 + 4 + 5 + 7
    c. 4 + 5 + 9
    d. 10 + 4 + 8

14. If an odd number is added to an even number, the result must be

    a. odd

    b. even

    c. positive

    d. zero

15. Which of the following numbers is greatest?

    a. 1/3

    b. 0.25

    c. 0.099

    d. 2/7

16. Bob spends $17.90 on sodas and snacks for his study group. The expenses are to be split evenly between five people. How much is each person's share?

    a. $3.45

    b. $3.58

    c. $3.65

    d. $3.73

17. A clothing store offers a red tag sale during which items are offered at 5% off the marked price. Margaret selects a dress with a marked price of $120. How much will she have to pay for it?

    a. $115

    b. $110

    c. $96

    d. $114

Answer Key and Explanations

Sentence Skills

1. C: The original sentence is redundant and wordy.

2. C: The syntax of the original sentence is fine, but a comma after *said* but before the open-quotation mark is required.

3. D: In the original sentence, the modifier is placed too far away from the word it modifies.

4. D: The verb structure should be consistent in a sentence with parallel structures.

5. A: The singular pronoun *her* is appropriate since the antecedents are joined by *or*. Also, the subjunctive verb form is required to indicate something indefinite.

6. B: The combination of *hardly* and *not* constitutes a double negative.

7. C: The plural demonstrative adjective *these* should be used with the plural noun *sorts*.

8. A: This sentence contains a number of parallel structures that must be treated consistently.

9. A: In this sentence, *whose* is the appropriate possessive pronoun to modify *opinion*.

10. B: Answer choice B is precise and clear. Answer choice A keeps the meaning, but is awkward and wordy. Answer choice C uses the wrong verb tense. Answer choice D would put the word *work* into the sentence twice. It is not completely incorrect, but it is not the best choice.

11. A: Answer choice A best completes statement in the rewritten sentence by making the immediate connection between the environmental concerns and the reason for them. Answer choice B could work within the context of the sentence, but it does not create a sufficient link between the environmental concerns and their causes. Answer choice C provides information that is not contained within the original sentence, and answer choice D also adds information by noting that the "delicate balance" is altered. While this might be inferred from the original sentence, it cannot be added to the rewritten sentence.

12. C: Answer choice C accurately adds the statement of contrast about the python being shorter in the wild. Answer choice A adds information to the original sentence. Answer choice B is technically correct but does not contain as much information as answer choice C and is thus not the best choice. Answer choice D is also technically correct but does not provide the substance of the information that answer choice C contains.

13. D: Answer choice D creates the necessary link between the snake owners and the infestation of pythons in the Everglades. Answer choice A contains accurate information, but the sentence does not flow smoothly from one idea to the next. Answer choice B is true but is vague and fails to create a sufficient link between ideas. Answer choice C contains details that make no sense within the context of the sentence.

14. A: Answer choice A provides the sense of contrast that is contained within the original sentence by showing the differences between the responsible snake owners and the lawmakers. Answer choice B offers information that is contained within the original sentence but fails to provide a clear

83

link between ideas. Answer choice C essentially repeats the information that is in the rewritten statement and is thus repetitive. Answer choice D, though correct, does not make a great deal of sense following up the information in the rewritten statement.

15. C: Answer choice C effectively restates the sentence by capturing the entire mood of the original. Answer choice A adds correct information, but it is incomplete with respect to the original idea. Answer choice B may be inferred to a degree, but there is not enough information in the original sentence to claim that the biologists were "surprised" about the results – only that they were "concerned" about the potential. Answer choice D adds information that is not within the original sentence.

16. A: Answer choice A correctly adds the necessary information about the alligator's traditional role within the Everglades. Answer choice B reassembles the information from the original sentence but does not provide the key detail about the alligator's place in the Everglades. Answer choices C and D add information that cannot be inferred from the original sentence.

17. B: Answer choice B provides the full information that is needed to complete the original idea. Answer choice A provides only partial information and is thus insufficient. Answer choice C is repetitive and does not offer any new information to complete the original idea. Answer choice D offers inferred information, but as this is not contained within the original sentence, it cannot be added.

18. D: Answer choice D adds the correct information about the concern that follows the python's expansion within the Everglades, without adding inferred information. Answer choice A is correct but is not necessarily effective in explaining the substance of the reason for concern. Answer choice B adds information that cannot be clearly inferred (i.e., what biologists and environmentalists originally believed about the python in the Everglades). Answer choice C adds information that has no place in the original sentence.

19. C: Answer choice C effectively links the ideas contained in the original sentence. Answer choice A is accurate but ineffective and incomplete, because it fails to explain *who* was doing the searching and destroying. Answer choices B and D add judgment statements that are not in the original sentence.

20. A: Answer choice A sufficiently links the ideas in the original sentence, connecting the reality of control with the hope for eradication. Answer choice B contradicts information that is not in the original sentence; that is to say, the original sentence states clearly that "eradication is preferred," not frowned upon. Answer choice C is partially correct but becomes incorrect with the added information about researchers continuing to search for means of eradication. Answer choice D contains correct information but does not encompass the full meaning of the original sentence and leaves out valuable information (i.e., the virtual impossibility of eradication).

Reading Comprehension

1. D: The passage states "Women are sold all sorts of creams and ointments and are promised that these will make them look younger over time. Unfortunately, these claims are entirely false. Lotions cannot penetrate to the inner layers of the skin, which is where wrinkles form." Therefore, these goods do not deliver what they promise.

2. B: The topic sentence is placed at the beginning of each supporting paragraph. Supporting evidence is presented after the topic sentence in each supporting paragraph. The passage states

"Next come the supporting paragraphs. Each paragraph contains a topic sentence, supporting evidence, and finally a type of mini-conclusion that restates the point of the paragraph."

3. D: The main idea discussed in the passage is that employers benefit the most from establishing a comfortable work space. The author points out that it is not extremely expensive, then identifies all of the benefits for employers: better productivity, less absenteeism, etc.

4. B: It can be concluded that many brides are choosing to wear colors other than white based on two statements in the passage. First, we know that bridesmaids do not wear the same color as the bride. Secondly, it is stated that white is a popular color for bridesmaid dresses. Therefore, since the color of the bridesmaid dress is not the same as the bride's dress, it can be concluded that the bride's dress is not white.

5. B: Many green fuels require more work to produce than conventional fuels. The passage states "producing natural gas is a much more labor-intensive process than producing an equal amount of conventional gasoline. Producing natural gas also involves burning fossil fuels."

6. C: This conclusion can be made based on two statements. First, the passage states that "the majority of crimes discussed on the nightly news featured African American suspects." Second, "it was found that white people were also suspects 50% of the time." Therefore, if half of all suspects are white, but the majority of suspects on the news are African American, it is reasonable to conclude that the news chooses not to report crimes that involve white suspects.

7. B: The main purpose of the passage is to discuss the possible benefits of stem cell research. The author states that many people feel it is unethical, but most of the passage is devoted to discussing the possible benefits of stem cell research. Cures for diseases and being able to repair spinal cord injuries are the possible benefits identified.

8. A: Accuracy is the same as correctness. The passage states "accuracy means that something is correct" and "if there was a glass of liquid that was 100 degrees, an accurate measurement would be one that was close to this temperature."

9. B: It can be concluded that phonics is a more effective way to learn to read for two reasons. First, the passage states that literacy rates are lower now than they were 15 years ago, meaning that more people knew how to read 15 years ago. Then, the passage states that phonics was the main way people learned how to read then. Therefore, based on these two facts, it can be concluded that phonics is more effective.

10. C: The passage states that "Shortly before becoming the President of the United States in 1789, Washington was an important leader in the American Revolutionary War from 1775 to 1783."

11. B: The second sentence explains the first by creating a link between the "period of administrative reform" and the failure at the Battle of Hakusukinoe. Answer choices A and D are incorrect, because the second sentence in no way undermines or refutes the first. Answer choice C is incorrect, because the second sentence does more than merely restate the first.

12. C: The second sentence clarifies the first by providing further detail about why the reform process in Japan "did not initially create the warrior system that later became the samurai." Answer choice A is incorrect, because it does not make sense in this context to say that the second sentence examines the first. Answer choice B is incorrect, because the second sentence does not just reaffirm the first: it provides further detail to explain the main point. Answer choice D is incorrect, because it limits the purpose of the second sentence. While the second sentence does indeed define a term, that is not its role. The second sentence clarifies the meaning of the first; in the process of doing so, it also happens to define a term.

13. B: The second sentence creates a conflict with the first, because the first sentence notes that the Emperor Kammu had a "serf army," while the second mentions his army of "clan members from his aristocracy." Without the historical explanation that Kammu dismissed the original army to create the aristocratic army, the second sentence appears to undermine the first. Answer choice A is incorrect, because instead of explaining the first sentence, the second sentence raises questions. Answer choice C is incorrect, because the second sentence could be said to require essential evidence but does not provide it. Answer choice D is incorrect, because it makes no sense in the context of the two sentences.

14. D: The second sentence implies a consequence: that the Emperor Kammu's power declined as a result of his choice to dismiss his aristocratic army. Answer choice A is incorrect, because the second sentence suggests a cause-and-effect relationship with the first, but this is not the same as presenting a new theory. (And without the context of what defines a new theory, answer choice A makes little sense.) Answer choice B is incorrect, because the second sentence seems to suggest a conclusion rather than the start of something new. Answer choice C is incorrect, because no context for crucial information is created between the two sentences.

15. C: The second sentence builds on the first by explaining how the aristocratic clans established themselves in Japanese culture by making marriages, creating treaties, and placing themselves under the Bushido. Answer choice A is incorrect, because it makes no sense in the context of the two sentences – no comparison is presented or made here. Answer choice B is incorrect, because no system is really classified; rather, the developing social position of the aristocratic clans is explained. Answer choice D is incorrect, because the second sentence supports and explains the main idea instead of refuting it.

16. A: As in question 5, the second sentence develops the primary idea of the first sentence by providing more detail about the Bushido and its meaning for the samurai. Answer choice B is incorrect, because it makes no sense; the possible effect is examined in the first sentence not the second if the Bushido were to be viewed as a type of cause. Answer choice C is incorrect, because no contrast is created within these sentences. Answer choice D is incorrect, because it describes the role of the first sentence instead of the second.

17. D: In the first sentence, a possible effect is created: the samurai became powerful during the late 12th century and the early 13th century. The second sentence follows with a mention of their success in a late 12th century battle. Therefore, the second sentence suggests a possible cause for the development of power. Answer choice A is incorrect, because it makes no sense in the context of the two sentences. Answer choice B is incorrect, because the second sentence does not attempt to question any part of the first. Answer choice C is incorrect, because no comparative information is offered in the second sentence.

18. B: The second sentence essentially restates the point of the first, that the samurai became more powerful than their lords and that the loyalty was largely in name-only by the end of the 13th century. Answer choice A is incorrect, because instead of undermining the main idea, the second sentence reaffirms it. In the same way, answer choice C is incorrect, because the second sentence does not counter, but rather confirm. Answer choice D is incorrect, because the role of the second sentence is to reiterate and not to examine.

19. C: The second sentence elaborates on the main idea by providing more information about what the samurai did since they were no longer needed as warriors. Answer choice A is incorrect, because the second sentence is not so much comparing as it is explaining. Answer choice B is incorrect, because the argument is established in the first sentence; the second sentence merely supports the argument. Answer choice D is incorrect, because it is difficult to determine within the limited context that is provided whether or not the information in the second sentence is "essential." The main idea is presented in the first sentence and could stand on its own. The second sentence simply adds supporting detail.

20. C: The second sentence suggests a cause-and-effect relationship that cannot be obviously inferred from the first but that can still follow as a possible result. The first sentence notes that many samurai struggled with the idea of death, and the second sentence indicates that the samurai practiced Zen Buddhism – which offers the very teachings that warriors might use to handle the potential for violent death. Answer choice A is incorrect, because no supporting information is brought to bear. Answer choice B is incorrect, because the first sentence does not offer a theory; instead, it states a fact. Answer choice D is incorrect, because the two sentences have a cause-and-effect relationship but not a compare-and-contrast relationship.

Arithmetic Test

1. A: 7 x 6 = 42. Dividing any of the other choices by 7 leaves a remainder. For example, 7 goes into 51 (choice C) 7 times (7 x 7 = 49), with 2 left over.

2. B: Percentage is equivalent to dividing by 100, so that $12.5\% = \frac{12.5}{100} = \frac{1}{8}$.

3. B: A prime number has only two whole integer divisors, 1 and itself. This is true of 3, 17, and 41. However 6 can be divided by 1, 2, 3, and 6. It is therefore not a prime number.

4. B: The reciprocal of 5 is $\frac{1}{5}$ When numbers are multiplied by their reciprocals, the result is always 1. Thus, $5 \times \frac{1}{5} = 1$.

5. D: To add mixed fractions, convert all the fractions so that they have the same denominator. This is done by finding the least common denominator, or LCD. In this case, since 8 equals 2 x 4, the LCD is 3 x 8 = 24. Now, convert all the fractions to a denominator of 24 by multiplying numerator and denominator by the same factors: $\frac{11(3)}{24} + \frac{7(24)}{24} + \frac{3(6)}{24} + \frac{4(8)}{24} = \frac{36+168+18+32}{24} = \frac{251}{24} = 10\frac{11}{24}$

6. A: The percentage of increase equals the change in the account balance divided by the original amount, $80, and multiplied by 100. First, determine the change in the balance by subtracting the original amount from the new balance: $Change = \$120 - \$80 = \$40$. Now, determine the percentage of increase as described above: $Percent = \frac{\$40}{\$80} \times 100 = 50\%$.

7. D: To round to 1/100, leave two digits to the right of the decimal. To round digits greater than 5, round up to the next value of the preceding digit.

8. B: Twenty percent of 70 is $\frac{20}{100} \times 70 = 14$. Three more than 14 is 3 + 14 = 17.

9. C: One half of 94 equals 47. Since 47 – 23 = 24, C is the correct answer.

10. B: To compute the average, first total all the items in the list and then divide by the number of items in the list. This yields $\frac{20+35+45+20}{4} = \frac{120}{4} = 30$. The difference between 45 and 30 is 15.

11. D: The area of a rectangle is calculated as the product of the width and length. If the length is twice the width of 3 m, it must be 6 m long. Then, 3 x 6 = 18 m².

12. C: The difference 27 – 23 = 4, and 300% of 4 is 3 times 4, or 12.

13. A: The sum 3 + 4 + 16 = 23. The other choices are less. In particular, although it has more terms, choice B, 6 + 4 + 5 + 7 = 22, which is less than choice A.

14. A: An odd number can be considered as an even number N plus 1. Two even numbers added together produce an even number, so the result of adding an odd and an even number must be an even number plus 1, which is odd. For example, 4 + 3 = 7.

15. A: Convert all the numbers to fractions and compare. The number 0.099 can be rounded to 0.1. Then, the first 3 choices are: a) 1/3; b) 1/4; c) 1/100. Since the numerators are equal, the number with the smallest denominator is greatest, and that is 1/3. To compare that with choice D, note that 1/3 = 2/6 and 2/6 > 2/7.

16. B: Since five people are dividing $17.90, each person's share is calculated as $\frac{17.90}{5} = 3.58$.

17. D: The price is reduced by an amount equal to 5% of the original price, or $\frac{5 \times \$120}{100} = \$6$, so subtract $6 from the original price of $120 to calculate the sale price: $114.

$$y(15) = -\frac{1}{2}(32)(15)^2 + 0 + 30{,}000 = -\frac{1}{2}(32)(225) + 0 + 30{,}000 = -3{,}600 + 30{,}000$$
$$= 26{,}400 \text{ft}$$

How to Overcome Test Anxiety

Just the thought of taking a test is enough to make most people a little nervous. A test is an important event that can have a long-term impact on your future, so it's important to take it seriously and it's natural to feel anxious about performing well. But just because anxiety is normal, that doesn't mean that it's helpful in test taking, or that you should simply accept it as part of your life. Anxiety can have a variety of effects. These effects can be mild, like making you feel slightly nervous, or severe, like blocking your ability to focus or remember even a simple detail.

If you experience test anxiety—whether severe or mild—it's important to know how to beat it. To discover this, first you need to understand what causes test anxiety.

Causes of Test Anxiety

While we often think of anxiety as an uncontrollable emotional state, it can actually be caused by simple, practical things. One of the most common causes of test anxiety is that a person does not feel adequately prepared for their test. This feeling can be the result of many different issues such as poor study habits or lack of organization, but the most common culprit is time management. Starting to study too late, failing to organize your study time to cover all of the material, or being distracted while you study will mean that you're not well prepared for the test. This may lead to cramming the night before, which will cause you to be physically and mentally exhausted for the test. Poor time management also contributes to feelings of stress, fear, and hopelessness as you realize you are not well prepared but don't know what to do about it.

Other times, test anxiety is not related to your preparation for the test but comes from unresolved fear. This may be a past failure on a test, or poor performance on tests in general. It may come from comparing yourself to others who seem to be performing better or from the stress of living up to expectations. Anxiety may be driven by fears of the future—how failure on this test would affect your educational and career goals. These fears are often completely irrational, but they can still negatively impact your test performance.

> **Review Video: 3 Reasons You Have Test Anxiety**
> Visit mometrix.com/academy and enter code: 428468

Elements of Test Anxiety

As mentioned earlier, test anxiety is considered to be an emotional state, but it has physical and mental components as well. Sometimes you may not even realize that you are suffering from test anxiety until you notice the physical symptoms. These can include trembling hands, rapid heartbeat, sweating, nausea, and tense muscles. Extreme anxiety may lead to fainting or vomiting. Obviously, any of these symptoms can have a negative impact on testing. It is important to recognize them as soon as they begin to occur so that you can address the problem before it damages your performance.

> **Review Video: 3 Ways to Tell You Have Test Anxiety**
> Visit mometrix.com/academy and enter code: 927847

The mental components of test anxiety include trouble focusing and inability to remember learned information. During a test, your mind is on high alert, which can help you recall information and stay focused for an extended period of time. However, anxiety interferes with your mind's natural processes, causing you to blank out, even on the questions you know well. The strain of testing during anxiety makes it difficult to stay focused, especially on a test that may take several hours. Extreme anxiety can take a huge mental toll, making it difficult not only to recall test information but even to understand the test questions or pull your thoughts together.

> **Review Video: How Test Anxiety Affects Memory**
> Visit mometrix.com/academy and enter code: 609003

Effects of Test Anxiety

Test anxiety is like a disease—if left untreated, it will get progressively worse. Anxiety leads to poor performance, and this reinforces the feelings of fear and failure, which in turn lead to poor performances on subsequent tests. It can grow from a mild nervousness to a crippling condition. If allowed to progress, test anxiety can have a big impact on your schooling, and consequently on your future.

Test anxiety can spread to other parts of your life. Anxiety on tests can become anxiety in any stressful situation, and blanking on a test can turn into panicking in a job situation. But fortunately, you don't have to let anxiety rule your testing and determine your grades. There are a number of relatively simple steps you can take to move past anxiety and function normally on a test and in the rest of life.

> **Review Video: How Test Anxiety Impacts Your Grades**
> Visit mometrix.com/academy and enter code: 939819

Physical Steps for Beating Test Anxiety

While test anxiety is a serious problem, the good news is that it can be overcome. It doesn't have to control your ability to think and remember information. While it may take time, you can begin taking steps today to beat anxiety.

Just as your first hint that you may be struggling with anxiety comes from the physical symptoms, the first step to treating it is also physical. Rest is crucial for having a clear, strong mind. If you are tired, it is much easier to give in to anxiety. But if you establish good sleep habits, your body and mind will be ready to perform optimally, without the strain of exhaustion. Additionally, sleeping well helps you to retain information better, so you're more likely to recall the answers when you see the test questions.

Getting good sleep means more than going to bed on time. It's important to allow your brain time to relax. Take study breaks from time to time so it doesn't get overworked, and don't study right before bed. Take time to rest your mind before trying to rest your body, or you may find it difficult to fall asleep.

> **Review Video: The Importance of Sleep for Your Brain**
> Visit mometrix.com/academy and enter code: 319338

Along with sleep, other aspects of physical health are important in preparing for a test. Good nutrition is vital for good brain function. Sugary foods and drinks may give a burst of energy but this burst is followed by a crash, both physically and emotionally. Instead, fuel your body with protein and vitamin-rich foods.

Also, drink plenty of water. Dehydration can lead to headaches and exhaustion, especially if your brain is already under stress from the rigors of the test. Particularly if your test is a long one, drink water during the breaks. And if possible, take an energy-boosting snack to eat between sections.

> **Review Video: How Diet Can Affect your Mood**
> Visit mometrix.com/academy and enter code: 624317

Along with sleep and diet, a third important part of physical health is exercise. Maintaining a steady workout schedule is helpful, but even taking 5-minute study breaks to walk can help get your blood pumping faster and clear your head. Exercise also releases endorphins, which contribute to a positive feeling and can help combat test anxiety.

When you nurture your physical health, you are also contributing to your mental health. If your body is healthy, your mind is much more likely to be healthy as well. So take time to rest, nourish your body with healthy food and water, and get moving as much as possible. Taking these physical steps will make you stronger and more able to take the mental steps necessary to overcome test anxiety.

Mental Steps for Beating Test Anxiety

Working on the mental side of test anxiety can be more challenging, but as with the physical side, there are clear steps you can take to overcome it. As mentioned earlier, test anxiety often stems from lack of preparation, so the obvious solution is to prepare for the test. Effective studying may be the most important weapon you have for beating test anxiety, but you can and should employ several other mental tools to combat fear.

First, boost your confidence by reminding yourself of past success—tests or projects that you aced. If you're putting as much effort into preparing for this test as you did for those, there's no reason you should expect to fail here. Work hard to prepare; then trust your preparation.

Second, surround yourself with encouraging people. It can be helpful to find a study group, but be sure that the people you're around will encourage a positive attitude. If you spend time with others who are anxious or cynical, this will only contribute to your own anxiety. Look for others who are motivated to study hard from a desire to succeed, not from a fear of failure.

Third, reward yourself. A test is physically and mentally tiring, even without anxiety, and it can be helpful to have something to look forward to. Plan an activity following the test, regardless of the outcome, such as going to a movie or getting ice cream.

When you are taking the test, if you find yourself beginning to feel anxious, remind yourself that you know the material. Visualize successfully completing the test. Then take a few deep, relaxing breaths and return to it. Work through the questions carefully but with confidence, knowing that you are capable of succeeding.

Developing a healthy mental approach to test taking will also aid in other areas of life. Test anxiety affects more than just the actual test—it can be damaging to your mental health and even contribute to depression. It's important to beat test anxiety before it becomes a problem for more than testing.

> **Review Video: Test Anxiety and Depression**
> Visit mometrix.com/academy and enter code: 904704

Study Strategy

Being prepared for the test is necessary to combat anxiety, but what does being prepared look like? You may study for hours on end and still not feel prepared. What you need is a strategy for test prep. The next few pages outline our recommended steps to help you plan out and conquer the challenge of preparation.

STEP 1: SCOPE OUT THE TEST

Learn everything you can about the format (multiple choice, essay, etc.) and what will be on the test. Gather any study materials, course outlines, or sample exams that may be available. Not only will this help you to prepare, but knowing what to expect can help to alleviate test anxiety.

STEP 2: MAP OUT THE MATERIAL

Look through the textbook or study guide and make note of how many chapters or sections it has. Then divide these over the time you have. For example, if a book has 15 chapters and you have five days to study, you need to cover three chapters each day. Even better, if you have the time, leave an extra day at the end for overall review after you have gone through the material in depth.

If time is limited, you may need to prioritize the material. Look through it and make note of which sections you think you already have a good grasp on, and which need review. While you are studying, skim quickly through the familiar sections and take more time on the challenging parts. Write out your plan so you don't get lost as you go. Having a written plan also helps you feel more in control of the study, so anxiety is less likely to arise from feeling overwhelmed at the amount to cover.

STEP 3: GATHER YOUR TOOLS

Decide what study method works best for you. Do you prefer to highlight in the book as you study and then go back over the highlighted portions? Or do you type out notes of the important information? Or is it helpful to make flashcards that you can carry with you? Assemble the pens, index cards, highlighters, post-it notes, and any other materials you may need so you won't be distracted by getting up to find things while you study.

If you're having a hard time retaining the information or organizing your notes, experiment with different methods. For example, try color-coding by subject with colored pens, highlighters, or post-it notes. If you learn better by hearing, try recording yourself reading your notes so you can listen while in the car, working out, or simply sitting at your desk. Ask a friend to quiz you from your flashcards, or try teaching someone the material to solidify it in your mind.

STEP 4: CREATE YOUR ENVIRONMENT

It's important to avoid distractions while you study. This includes both the obvious distractions like visitors and the subtle distractions like an uncomfortable chair (or a too-comfortable couch that makes you want to fall asleep). Set up the best study environment possible: good lighting and a comfortable work area. If background music helps you focus, you may want to turn it on, but otherwise keep the room quiet. If you are using a computer to take notes, be sure you don't have any other windows open, especially applications like social media, games, or anything else that could distract you. Silence your phone and turn off notifications. Be sure to keep water close by so you stay hydrated while you study (but avoid unhealthy drinks and snacks).

Also, take into account the best time of day to study. Are you freshest first thing in the morning? Try to set aside some time then to work through the material. Is your mind clearer in the afternoon or evening? Schedule your study session then. Another method is to study at the same time of day that you will take the test, so that your brain gets used to working on the material at that time and will be ready to focus at test time.

STEP 5: STUDY!

Once you have done all the study preparation, it's time to settle into the actual studying. Sit down, take a few moments to settle your mind so you can focus, and begin to follow your study plan. Don't give in to distractions or let yourself procrastinate. This is your time to prepare so you'll be ready to fearlessly approach the test. Make the most of the time and stay focused.

Of course, you don't want to burn out. If you study too long you may find that you're not retaining the information very well. Take regular study breaks. For example, taking five minutes out of every hour to walk briskly, breathing deeply and swinging your arms, can help your mind stay fresh.

As you get to the end of each chapter or section, it's a good idea to do a quick review. Remind yourself of what you learned and work on any difficult parts. When you feel that you've mastered the material, move on to the next part. At the end of your study session, briefly skim through your notes again.

But while review is helpful, cramming last minute is NOT. If at all possible, work ahead so that you won't need to fit all your study into the last day. Cramming overloads your brain with more information than it can process and retain, and your tired mind may struggle to recall even previously learned information when it is overwhelmed with last-minute study. Also, the urgent nature of cramming and the stress placed on your brain contribute to anxiety. You'll be more likely to go to the test feeling unprepared and having trouble thinking clearly.

So don't cram, and don't stay up late before the test, even just to review your notes at a leisurely pace. Your brain needs rest more than it needs to go over the information again. In fact, plan to finish your studies by noon or early afternoon the day before the test. Give your brain the rest of the day to relax or focus on other things, and get a good night's sleep. Then you will be fresh for the test and better able to recall what you've studied.

STEP 6: TAKE A PRACTICE TEST

Many courses offer sample tests, either online or in the study materials. This is an excellent resource to check whether you have mastered the material, as well as to prepare for the test format and environment.

Check the test format ahead of time: the number of questions, the type (multiple choice, free response, etc.), and the time limit. Then create a plan for working through them. For example, if you have 30 minutes to take a 60-question test, your limit is 30 seconds per question. Spend less time on the questions you know well so that you can take more time on the difficult ones.

If you have time to take several practice tests, take the first one open book, with no time limit. Work through the questions at your own pace and make sure you fully understand them. Gradually work up to taking a test under test conditions: sit at a desk with all study materials put away and set a timer. Pace yourself to make sure you finish the test with time to spare and go back to check your answers if you have time.

After each test, check your answers. On the questions you missed, be sure you understand why you missed them. Did you misread the question (tests can use tricky wording)? Did you forget the information? Or was it something you hadn't learned? Go back and study any shaky areas that the practice tests reveal.

Taking these tests not only helps with your grade, but also aids in combating test anxiety. If you're already used to the test conditions, you're less likely to worry about it, and working through tests until you're scoring well gives you a confidence boost. Go through the practice tests until you feel comfortable, and then you can go into the test knowing that you're ready for it.

Test Tips

On test day, you should be confident, knowing that you've prepared well and are ready to answer the questions. But aside from preparation, there are several test day strategies you can employ to maximize your performance.

First, as stated before, get a good night's sleep the night before the test (and for several nights before that, if possible). Go into the test with a fresh, alert mind rather than staying up late to study.

Try not to change too much about your normal routine on the day of the test. It's important to eat a nutritious breakfast, but if you normally don't eat breakfast at all, consider eating just a protein bar. If you're a coffee drinker, go ahead and have your normal coffee. Just make sure you time it so that the caffeine doesn't wear off right in the middle of your test. Avoid sugary beverages, and drink enough water to stay hydrated but not so much that you need a restroom break 10 minutes into the test. If your test isn't first thing in the morning, consider going for a walk or doing a light workout before the test to get your blood flowing.

Allow yourself enough time to get ready, and leave for the test with plenty of time to spare so you won't have the anxiety of scrambling to arrive in time. Another reason to be early is to select a good seat. It's helpful to sit away from doors and windows, which can be distracting. Find a good seat, get out your supplies, and settle your mind before the test begins.

When the test begins, start by going over the instructions carefully, even if you already know what to expect. Make sure you avoid any careless mistakes by following the directions.

Then begin working through the questions, pacing yourself as you've practiced. If you're not sure on an answer, don't spend too much time on it, and don't let it shake your confidence. Either skip it and come back later, or eliminate as many wrong answers as possible and guess among the remaining ones. Don't dwell on these questions as you continue—put them out of your mind and focus on what lies ahead.

Be sure to read all of the answer choices, even if you're sure the first one is the right answer. Sometimes you'll find a better one if you keep reading. But don't second-guess yourself if you do immediately know the answer. Your gut instinct is usually right. Don't let test anxiety rob you of the information you know.

If you have time at the end of the test (and if the test format allows), go back and review your answers. Be cautious about changing any, since your first instinct tends to be correct, but make sure you didn't misread any of the questions or accidentally mark the wrong answer choice. Look over any you skipped and make an educated guess.

At the end, leave the test feeling confident. You've done your best, so don't waste time worrying about your performance or wishing you could change anything. Instead, celebrate the successful

completion of this test. And finally, use this test to learn how to deal with anxiety even better next time.

Important Qualification

Not all anxiety is created equal. If your test anxiety is causing major issues in your life beyond the classroom or testing center, or if you are experiencing troubling physical symptoms related to your anxiety, it may be a sign of a serious physiological or psychological condition. If this sounds like your situation, we strongly encourage you to seek professional help.

How to Overcome Your Fear of Math

Not again. You're sitting in math class, look down at your test, and immediately start to panic. Your stomach is in knots, your heart is racing, and you break out in a cold sweat. You're staring at the paper, but everything looks like it's written in a foreign language. Even though you studied, you're blanking out on how to begin solving these problems.

Does this sound familiar? If so, then you're not alone! You may be like millions of other people who experience math anxiety. Anxiety about performing well in math is a common experience for students of all ages. In this article, we'll discuss what math anxiety is, common misconceptions about learning math, and tips and strategies for overcoming math anxiety.

What Is Math Anxiety?

Psychologist Mark H. Ashcraft explains math anxiety as a feeling of tension, apprehension, or fear that interferes with math performance. Having math anxiety negatively impacts people's beliefs about themselves and what they can achieve. It hinders achievement within the math classroom and affects the successful application of mathematics in the real world.

SYMPTOMS AND SIGNS OF MATH ANXIETY

To overcome math anxiety, you must recognize its symptoms. Becoming aware of the signs of math anxiety is the first step in addressing and resolving these fears.

NEGATIVE SELF-TALK

If you have math anxiety, you've most likely said at least one of these statements to yourself:

- "I hate math."
- "I'm not good at math."
- "I'm not a math person."

The way we speak to ourselves and think about ourselves matters. Our thoughts become our words, our words become our actions, and our actions become our habits. Thinking negatively about math creates a self-fulfilling prophecy. In other words, if you take an idea as a fact, then it will come true because your behaviors will align to match it.

AVOIDANCE

Some people who are fearful or anxious about math will tend to avoid it altogether. Avoidance can manifest in the following ways:

- Lack of engagement with math content
- Not completing homework and other assignments
- Not asking for help when needed
- Skipping class
- Avoiding math-related courses and activities

Avoidance is one of the most harmful impacts of math anxiety. If you steer clear of math at all costs, then you can't set yourself up for the success you deserve.

LACK OF MOTIVATION

Students with math anxiety may experience a lack of motivation. They may struggle to find the incentive to get engaged with what they view as a frightening subject. These students are often overwhelmed, making it difficult for them to complete or even start math assignments.

PROCRASTINATION

Another symptom of math anxiety is procrastination. Students may voluntarily delay or postpone their classwork and assignments, even if they know there will be a negative consequence for doing so. Additionally, they may choose to wait until the last minute to start projects and homework, even when they know they need more time to put forth their best effort.

PHYSIOLOGICAL REACTIONS

Many people with a fear of math experience physiological side effects. These may include an increase in heart rate, sweatiness, shakiness, nausea, and irregular breathing. These symptoms make it difficult to focus on the math content, causing the student even more stress and fear.

STRONG EMOTIONAL RESPONSES

Math anxiety also affects people on an emotional level. Responding to math content with strong emotions such as panic, anger, or despair can be a sign of math anxiety.

LOW TEST SCORES AND PERFORMANCE

Low achievement can be both a symptom and a cause of math anxiety. When someone does not take the steps needed to perform well on tests and assessments, they are less likely to pass. The more they perform poorly, the more they accept this poor performance as a fact that can't be changed.

FEELING ALONE

People who experience math anxiety feel like they are the only ones struggling, even if the math they are working on is challenging to many people. Feeling isolated in what they perceive as failure can trigger tension or nervousness.

FEELING OF PERMANENCY

Math anxiety can feel very permanent. You may assume that you are naturally bad at math and always will be. Viewing math as a natural ability rather than a skill that can be learned causes people to believe that nothing will help them improve. They take their current math abilities as fact and assume that they can't be changed. As a result, they give up, stop trying to improve, and avoid engaging with math altogether.

LACK OF CONFIDENCE

People with low self-confidence in math tend to feel awkward and incompetent when asked to solve a math problem. They don't feel comfortable taking chances or risks when problem-solving because they second-guess themselves and assume they are incorrect. They don't trust in their ability to learn the content and solve problems correctly.

PANIC

A general sense of unexplained panic is also a sign of math anxiety. You may feel a sudden sense of fear that triggers physical reactions, even when there is no apparent reason for such a response.

CAUSES OF MATH ANXIETY

Math anxiety can start at a young age and may have one or more underlying causes. Common causes of math anxiety include the following:

THE ATTITUDE OF PARENTS OR GUARDIANS

Parents often put pressure on their children to perform well in school. Although their intentions are usually good, this pressure can lead to anxiety, especially if the student is struggling with a subject or class.

Perhaps your parents or others in your life hold negative predispositions about math based on their own experiences. For instance, if your mother once claimed she was not good at math, then you might have incorrectly interpreted this as a predisposed trait that was passed down to you.

TEACHER INFLUENCE

Students often pick up on their teachers' attitudes about the content being taught. If a teacher is happy and excited about math, students are more likely to mirror these emotions. However, if a teacher lacks enthusiasm or genuine interest, then students are more inclined to disengage.

Teachers have a responsibility to cultivate a welcoming classroom culture that is accepting of mistakes. When teachers blame students for not understanding a concept, they create a hostile classroom environment where mistakes are not tolerated. This tension increases student stress and anxiety, creating conditions that are not conducive to inquiry and learning. Instead, when teachers normalize mistakes as a natural part of the problem-solving process, they give their students the freedom to explore and grapple with the math content. In such an environment, students feel comfortable taking chances because they are not afraid of being wrong.

Students need teachers that can help when they're having problems understanding difficult concepts. In doing so, educators may need to change how they teach the content. Since different people have unique learning styles, it's the job of the teacher to adapt to the needs of each student. Additionally, teachers should encourage students to explore alternate problem-solving strategies, even if it's not the preferred method of the educator.

FEAR OF BEING WRONG

Embarrassing situations can be traumatic, especially for young children and adolescents. These experiences can stay with people through their adult lives. Those with math anxiety may experience a fear of being wrong, especially in front of a group of peers. This fear can be paralyzing, interfering with the student's concentration and ability to focus on the problem at hand.

TIMED ASSESSMENTS

Timed assessments can help improve math fluency, but they often create unnecessary pressure for students to complete an unrealistic number of problems within a specified timeframe. Many studies have shown that timed assessments often result in increased levels of anxiety, reducing a student's overall competence and ability to problem-solve.

Debunking Math Myths

There are lots of myths about math that are related to the causes and development of math-related anxiety. Although these myths have been proven to be false, many people take them as fact. Let's go over a few of the most common myths about learning math.

MYTH: MEN ARE BETTER AT MATH THAN WOMEN

Math has a reputation for being a male-dominant subject, but this doesn't mean that men are inherently better at math than women. Many famous mathematical discoveries have been made by women. Katherine Johnson, Dame Mary Lucy Cartwright, and Marjorie Lee Brown are just a few of the many famous women mathematicians. Expecting to be good or bad at math because of your gender sets you up for stress and confusion. Math is a skill that can be learned, just like cooking or riding a bike.

MYTH: THERE IS ONLY ONE GOOD WAY TO SOLVE MATH PROBLEMS

There are many ways to get the correct answer when it comes to math. No two people have the same brain, so everyone takes a slightly different approach to problem-solving. Moreover, there isn't one way of problem-solving that's superior to another. Your way of working through a problem might differ from someone else's, and that is okay. Math can be a highly individualized process, so the best method for you should be the one that makes you feel the most comfortable and makes the most sense to you.

MYTH: MATH REQUIRES A GOOD MEMORY

For many years, mathematics was taught through memorization. However, learning in such a way hinders the development of critical thinking and conceptual understanding. These skill sets are much more valuable than basic memorization. For instance, you might be great at memorizing mathematical formulas, but if you don't understand what they mean, then you can't apply them to different scenarios in the real world. When a student is working from memory, they are limited in the strategies available to them to problem-solve. In other words, they assume there is only one correct way to do the math, which is the method they memorized. Having a variety of problem-solving options can help students figure out which method works best for them. Additionally, it provides students with a better understanding of how and why certain mathematical strategies work. While memorization can be helpful in some instances, it is not an absolute requirement for mathematicians.

MYTH: MATH IS NOT CREATIVE

Math requires imagination and intuition. Contrary to popular belief, it is a highly creative field. Mathematical creativity can help in developing new ways to think about and solve problems. Many people incorrectly assume that all things are either creative or analytical. However, this black-and-white view is limiting because the field of mathematics involves both creativity and logic.

MYTH: MATH ISN'T SUPPOSED TO BE FUN

Whoever told you that math isn't supposed to be fun is a liar. There are tons of math-based activities and games that foster friendly competition and engagement. Math is often best learned through play, and lots of mobile apps and computer games exemplify this.

Additionally, math can be an exceptionally collaborative and social experience. Studying or working through problems with a friend often makes the process a lot more fun. The excitement and satisfaction of solving a difficult problem with others is quite rewarding. Math can be fun if you look for ways to make it more collaborative and enjoyable.

MYTH: NOT EVERYONE IS CAPABLE OF LEARNING MATH

There's no such thing as a "math person." Although many people think that you're either good at math or you're not, this is simply not true. Everyone is capable of learning and applying mathematics. However, not everyone learns the same way. Since each person has a different learning style, the trick is to find the strategies and learning tools that work best for you. Some people learn best through hands-on experiences, and others find success through the use of visual aids. Others are auditory learners and learn best by hearing and listening. When people are overwhelmed or feel that math is too hard, it's often because they haven't found the learning strategy that works best for them.

MYTH: GOOD MATHEMATICIANS WORK QUICKLY AND NEVER MAKE MISTAKES

There is no prize for finishing first in math. It's not a race, and speed isn't a measure of your ability. Good mathematicians take their time to ensure their work is accurate. As you gain more experience and practice, you will naturally become faster and more confident.

Additionally, everyone makes mistakes, including good mathematicians. Mistakes are a normal part of the problem-solving process, and they're not a bad thing. The important thing is that we take the time to learn from our mistakes, understand where our misconceptions are, and move forward.

MYTH: YOU DON'T NEED MATH IN THE REAL WORLD

Our day-to-day lives are so infused with mathematical concepts that we often don't even realize when we're using math in the real world. In fact, most people tend to underestimate how much we do math in our everyday lives. It's involved in an enormous variety of daily activities such as shopping, baking, finances, and gardening, as well as in many careers, including architecture, nursing, design, and sales.

Tips and Strategies for Overcoming Math Anxiety

If your anxiety is getting in the way of your level of mathematical engagement, then there are lots of steps you can take. Check out the strategies below to start building confidence in math today.

FOCUS ON UNDERSTANDING, NOT MEMORIZATION

Don't drive yourself crazy trying to memorize every single formula or mathematical process. Instead, shift your attention to understanding concepts. Those who prioritize memorization over conceptual understanding tend to have lower achievement levels in math. Students who memorize may be able to complete some math, but they don't understand the process well enough to apply it to different situations. Memorization comes with time and practice, but it won't help alleviate math anxiety. On the other hand, conceptual understanding will give you the building blocks of knowledge you need to build up your confidence.

REPLACE NEGATIVE SELF-TALK WITH POSITIVE SELF-TALK

Start to notice how you think about yourself. Whenever you catch yourself thinking something negative, try replacing that thought with a positive affirmation. Instead of continuing the negative thought, pause to reframe the situation. For ideas on how to get started, take a look at the table below:

Instead of thinking...	Try thinking...
"I can't do this math." "I'm not a math person."	"I'm up for the challenge, and I'm training my brain in math."
"This problem is too hard."	"This problem is hard, so this might take some time and effort. I know I can do this."
"I give up."	"What strategies can help me solve this problem?"
"I made a mistake, so I'm not good at this."	"Everyone makes mistakes. Mistakes help me to grow and understand."
"I'll never be smart enough."	"I can figure this out, and I am smart enough."

PRACTICE MINDFULNESS

Practicing mindfulness and focusing on your breathing can help alleviate some of the physical symptoms of math anxiety. By taking deep breaths, you can remind your nervous system that you are not in immediate danger. Doing so will reduce your heart rate and help with any irregular breathing or shakiness. Taking the edge off of the physiological effects of anxiety will clear your mind, allowing your brain to focus its energy on problem-solving.

DO SOME MATH EVERY DAY

Think about learning math as if you were learning a foreign language. If you don't use it, you lose it. If you don't practice your math skills regularly, you'll have a harder time achieving comprehension and fluency. Set some amount of time aside each day, even if it's just for a few minutes, to practice. It might take some discipline to build a habit around this, but doing so will help increase your mathematical self-assurance.

USE ALL OF YOUR RESOURCES

Everyone has a different learning style, and there are plenty of resources out there to support all learners. When you get stuck on a math problem, think about the tools you have access to, and use them when applicable. Such resources may include flashcards, graphic organizers, study guides, interactive notebooks, and peer study groups. All of these are great tools to accommodate your individual learning style. Finding the tools and resources that work for your learning style will give you the confidence you need to succeed.

REALIZE THAT YOU AREN'T ALONE

Remind yourself that lots of other people struggle with math anxiety, including teachers, nurses, and even successful mathematicians. You aren't the only one who panics when faced with a new or challenging problem. It's probably much more common than you think. Realizing that you aren't alone in your experience can help put some distance between yourself and the emotions you feel about math. It also helps to normalize the anxiety and shift your perspective.

ASK QUESTIONS

If there's a concept you don't understand and you've tried everything you can, then it's okay to ask for help! You can always ask your teacher or professor for help. If you're not learning math in a traditional classroom, you may want to join a study group, work with a tutor, or talk to your friends. More often than not, you aren't the only one of your peers who needs clarity on a mathematical concept. Seeking understanding is a great way to increase self-confidence in math.

REMEMBER THAT THERE'S MORE THAN ONE WAY TO SOLVE A PROBLEM

Since everyone learns differently, it's best to focus on understanding a math problem with an approach that makes sense to you. If the way it's being taught is confusing to you, don't give up. Instead, work to understand the problem using a different technique. There's almost always more than one problem-solving method when it comes to math. Don't get stressed if one of them doesn't make sense to you. Instead, shift your focus to what does make sense. Chances are high that you know more than you think you do.

VISUALIZATION

Visualization is the process of creating images in your mind's eye. Picture yourself as a successful, confident mathematician. Think about how you would feel and how you would behave. What would your work area look like? How would you organize your belongings? The more you focus on something, the more likely you are to achieve it. Visualizing teaches your brain that you can achieve whatever it is that you want. Thinking about success in mathematics will lead to acting like a successful mathematician. This, in turn, leads to actual success.

FOCUS ON THE EASIEST PROBLEMS FIRST

To increase your confidence when working on a math test or assignment, try solving the easiest problems first. Doing so will remind you that you are successful in math and that you do have what it takes. This process will increase your belief in yourself, giving you the confidence you need to tackle more complex problems.

FIND A SUPPORT GROUP

A study buddy, tutor, or peer group can go a long way in decreasing math-related anxiety. Such support systems offer lots of benefits, including a safe place to ask questions, additional practice with mathematical concepts, and an understanding of other problem-solving explanations that may work better for you. Equipping yourself with a support group is one of the fastest ways to eliminate math anxiety.

REWARD YOURSELF FOR WORKING HARD

Recognize the amount of effort you're putting in to overcome your math anxiety. It's not an easy task, so you deserve acknowledgement. Surround yourself with people who will provide you with the positive reinforcement you deserve.

Remember, You Can Do This!

Conquering a fear of math can be challenging, but there are lots of strategies that can help you out. Your own beliefs about your mathematical capabilities can limit your potential. Working toward a growth mindset can have a tremendous impact on decreasing math-related anxiety and building confidence. By knowing the symptoms of math anxiety and recognizing common misconceptions about learning math, you can develop a plan to address your fear of math. Utilizing the strategies discussed can help you overcome this anxiety and build the confidence you need to succeed.

Thank You

We at Mometrix would like to extend our heartfelt thanks to you, our friend and patron, for allowing us to play a part in your journey. It is a privilege to serve people from all walks of life who are unified in their commitment to building the best future they can for themselves.

The preparation you devote to these important testing milestones may be the most valuable educational opportunity you have for making a real difference in your life. We encourage you to put your heart into it—that feeling of succeeding, overcoming, and yes, conquering will be well worth the hours you've invested.

We want to hear your story, your struggles and your successes, and if you see any opportunities for us to improve our materials so we can help others even more effectively in the future, please share that with us as well. **The team at Mometrix would be absolutely thrilled to hear from you!** So please, send us an email (support@mometrix.com) and let's stay in touch.

> **If you'd like some additional help, check out these other resources we offer for your exam:**
> **http://MometrixFlashcards.com/ATB**

Additional Bonus Material

Due to our efforts to try to keep this book to a manageable length, we've created a link that will give you access to all of your additional bonus material:

mometrix.com/bonus948/atb